MAIN STREET
VERSUS
WALL STREET

Transforming Raw Anger
Into Purposeful Action

JOHN F. INCE

Published by:

The Serendigity Publishing Group

Email: info@serendigity.com

ISBN-13: 978-1468053906

ISBN-10: 1468053906

To join with others concerned about general issues
raised in this book visit:
www.MeaningfulMoney.net

To join a conversation about *The Money Question* visit:
www.Money-Question.net

To order additional copies of this book visit:
www.Money-Question.com

To read John F. Ince's blog visit: www.JohnInce.com

To follow *The Money Question* on Twitter visit:
http://twitter.com/moneyquestion

For additional information or for discounts on bulk orders of this book
email: Info@Money-Question.com

***

THIS BOOK IS DEDICATED TO THOSE WHO ARE OUT THERE IN THE STREETS RAISING AWARENESS OF A SYSTEM THAT NEEDS TO BE FIXED.

***

Acknowledgements

Writing this book will not have been possible without the support, input, ideas and insight from the following people: Chris Anderson, Author and Editor of *Wired Magazine*; Marc Andreessen, Internet Entrepreneur and Investor; Peter Barnes, Author, Capitalism 3.0; Robert Sheer, Columnist; Robert Johnson, Kenneth Larsen; Wayne Baker, Author, *Achieving Success Through Social Capital*; William Baue, *Sustainability Investment News*; Ellen Brown, Author: *The Web of Debt*; Leslie Berlin, Blogger; Tim Beyers; Richard Cashin, Managing Partner, One Equity Partners; Adam Cherier, Filmmaker and Book Editor; Clifford Cobb, co-author of *If the GDP is Up, Why is America Down?*; Marc Dangeard, Founder, Entrepreneur Commons; Liana DeBare, *The San Francisco Chronicle*; Joe Dominguez, Co-author, *Your Money or Your Life*; Jed Emerson, Uruhu Capital; James Fallows, National Editor, *The Atlantic Monthly*; Niall Ferguson, Author and HBS Professor; Steve Fraser, Writer; Edward Hadas - Editor, *Fortune Magazine*; Donald Gogel, Managing Partner, Clayton, Dubilier & Rice, Inc.; Paul Glover, Founder, Ithaca Hours; Thomas H. Greco, Jr. Author, *The End of Money and the Future of Civilization* William Greider, Author, *Secrets of the Temple: How the Federal Reserve Runs the Country*; Paul Haller, Teacher of "The Dharma of Money" at The San Francisco Zen Center; Ted Halstead, Founder, New America Foundation and co-author of *If the GDP is Up, Why is America Down? in The Atlantic in October 1995*; Charles Handy, *Harvard Business Review,* Arianna Huffington, Blogger, *The Huffington Post*; Carla Javits, President, REDF; Simon Johnson, Former Chief Economist, IMF; James Kouzes, Chair Emeritus of Tom Peters Company; Paul Krugman Economist; Bob Ivry, *Bloomberg*; John Kemp, Author of *U.S. & UK on Brink of Debt Disaster*; Mark Knoller, *CBS News*; Paul Lamb, Principal of Man on a Mission Consulting, Tim Leberecht, CNET News - Matter/Anti-Matter; Matt Lawlor, CEO, Online Resources; Bernard Lietaer, Author, *The Future of Money*; Michael Linton, *Local Exchange Trading Systems*; Lou Michaels, Author, *The Rainmaker, Thinking Outside the Box*; William R. Neil, Writer; Floyd Norris, Financial Columnist, *The New York Times*; Mark Pittman, *Bloomberg*; Vicki Robin, Co-author of *Your Money or Your Life*; Jonathan Rowe, Co-author of *Time Dollars* and *If the GDP is Up, Why is America Down?*; Tom Raum, Washington Office of the Associated Press, Mark Scott, Writer for *Business Week*; Howard Rheingold, Author, *The Future of Money*; Joseph Stiglitz, Nobel Prize-winning economist; Will Thompson, Thompson Doorman; Andy Tobias, Author; Nick Turse Blogger ; George Soros, Author and Investor; Joseph Stiglitz, Economist and Nobel Laureate; Amie Vaquero, Director of Business Development for Viv;

Other Books by John F. Ince

MAIN STREET VERSUS WALL STREET: CHANGING THE SYSTEM - The System is broken, but how do we fix it? Capitalism is in the midst of an identity crisis. Very few take issue with the capitalism in its ideal form, but the system has morphed into a dragon that few people want to defend. It has become a grotesque form of something that

COMMON CENTS: NEW MONEY VS OLD MONEY AND THE NEXT AMERICAN REVOLUTION - Our world finds itself on the brink of an unprecedented crisis of an epic proportions, distinguished by the fact that so many sectors of society are simultaneously feeling its wrath. Many times in history the world has faced crises but never have they been of such magnitude and never before have so many of our most fundamental assumptions and institutions

MEANINGFUL MONEY: INNOVATION AT THE INTERSECTION OF MEANING, MONEY AND MARKETS - The root cause of our crises lies nowhere else but in our modes of thinking and these modes have become so deeply ingrained into our thinking. We are in drift mode, and we all suffer from the same disfunction: tunnel vision.

Table of Contents

Fixing A Broken System

The system is broken and to fix it we need a game changer. No quick fixes … no more smoke and mirrors. We need a bold vision and new model to change the system. Big job! Changing the system is hard work. Whether it be on a personal or societal level, we know we must change, but we're anxious about the uncertainty of the future. So we construct all kinds of false reasons why we can continue with what we know isn't working, often enduring pain while force of inertia prevails for a while longer. Finally a reckoning comes upon us and we no longer have a choice. We must accept the change that the evolutionary process has been politely suggesting to us for so long. When we're forced to change in this way,  it becomes acutely painful, sometimes excruciating. If instead we anticipate trends, we can make change our friend. I do not underestimate the force of institutional inertia that stands in the way of meaningful change in our money and banking system. It is the very foundation of our entire economy. Powerful forces are arrayed against change, but more powerful forces are coming to the fore. These forces go deep into our history and consciousness.

What Is the Next Phase of Occupy Wall Street?

Occupy Wall Street may be facing a fork in the road as the protest movement wrestles with how to become a more effective political force.

The tension between achieving reforms through protests and promoting a deeper revolution is evident in intense debates and discussions that take place outside the park in churches and at an atrium at 60 Wall Street, a public space next to the Deutsche Bank building.

So at various points in the days, bankers leaving their offices unknowingly walk by intense circles of people in far funkier and more practical clothing huddled into circles to discuss strategies and tactics in work groups operating on principles of open discussion an effort to find consensus.

Some activists are critical of too much internal discourse and not enough external outreach, especially to the communities hardest hit by the economic crisis. There are many meetings about coordination, facilitation and a 'spokescouncil' that could supplant their open-to-all General Assembly.

Many are aware that the movement's current base may not be more than 1 percent of the 99 percent they march in the name of. Maybe even less. They know that their chances of securing the changes they want are tied to creating campaigns and organizing strategies that are less counter-cultural and more political, campaigns that can mobilize workers, communities of color and campuses struggling under the weight of student debt and beak futures in the job market. This takes toning town some of the rhetoric political style that drives the movement. ... Can it build organizations that people can join -- and identify with?

At the moment, these "leaderless" activists see this approach as more manipulative than participatory but how else can they convince people unlike themselves -- people without histories of radical political activism or union militancy to feel comfortable in a youth dominated harder-edge movement with its unique mix of direct activism and small "d" democratic idealism? Occupy is very strong when it comes to creative tactics, but what is the longer-term strategy? How will it have a change to shape and implement one?

- Danny Schechter - Editor, MediaChannel.org

Mainstreaming "The Movement"

This book is an attempt to start the conversation that can lead to a plan for systemic change. This book is about "Mainstreaming the Movement." Notice I didn't say mainstreaming the Occupy Wall Street Movement, or the Tea Party Movement or any other specific movement.

The Occupy Wall Street Movement has dismissed the Tea Party as a fringe group on the right. The Tea Party Movement has dismissed Occupy Wall Street as a fringe group on the left. Actually both groups ... and many others are fighting for the same thing: economic fairness ... economic democracy ... the right to earn their fair share from the system that today disproportionately rewards the haves at the expense of the have nots.

These movement don't have visible leaders. These movements don't have an agenda. But there is one thing that unites all these movements: a deeply held and spreading conviction that we're all getting screwed by the system. Something isn't fair about the way economic power is distributed in our society. The system is rigged. Democracy hasn't fulfilled it's promise ... democracy hasn't lived up to the hype. People want to be acknowledged. People want to be part of the conversation.

Wall Street's reply? "What are you going to do about it?
That's the question isn't it. That's the question that underlies all the protests ... all the talk ... all the posturing ... all the occupying ...

What are we going to do about it?

THEY CAN'T BEAT DOWN HOPES, DREAMS AND THE FIGHT FOR A MORE HUMANE WORLD

WHO KNEW, OR COULD EVEN IMAGINE, THAT IN SUCH A SHORT TIME, THE OCCUPY WALL STREET MOVEMENT WOULD INSPIRE A STRIKING TRANSFORMATION OF PUBLIC CONSCIOUSNESS, CAPTURING THE IMAGINATION OF THE COUNTRY AND THE GLOBE, AND FUNDAMENTALLY CHANGING THE PUBLIC DISCOURSE? AND IT'S JUST THE BEGINNING...

THIS IS AN OPPORTUNITY FOR A TRANSCENDENT MOMENT. ...

WE ARE A SOCIETY THAT DESERVES AND WILL IN THE END ACHIEVE SOMETHING MUCH BETTER, MORE HUMANE AND MORE SANE THAN WHAT WE HAVE NOW.

THERE IS NO PUTTING THIS GENIE BACK IN THE BOTTLE. SO NEW YORKERS AND PROTESTERS AND THEIR ALLIES AND FRIENDS ACROSS THE COUNTRY AND GLOBE: TAKE A DEEP BREATH. THERE IS A LONG ROAD AHEAD, BUT EVERY DAY AND EVERY OBSTACLE OVERCOME LEADS TO A BETTER TOMORROW. WE JUST HAVE TO STAY STRONG AND REFUSE TO TAKE NO FOR AN ANSWER.

ALTERNET / BY DON HAZEN - NOVEMBER 15, 2011

Trust in Our Institutions is Eroding

Something of profound significance is unfolding with the confluence of major trends:
• the anti-Wall Street protests,
• American economic malaise,
• European Debt Crisis,
• technological innovation,
• political paralysis.

For millennia, trust in governments has been the is the foundation of all national and

international money systems.

But today, our trust in governments is eroding ... seriously eroding ... to the point where the the trust we place in both our government and our banking system is threatening the money system itself. In other works the code of the global operating system has been exposed as faulty.

The questions before us now are:
• Can a new kind of trust coalesce in a new kind of money and banking system?
• Can we rewrite that code to make a parallel system that is more sustainable?
• Can we seize this opportunity to create genuine economic democracy?
• What might a new money and banking system look like?

This is the inquiry of this book, extrapolating from major trends in finance, technology, popular dissent and politics to catch a glimpse of a better way of thinking about the most powerful tool every created by humans–money.

"The end of democracy and the defeat of the American Revolution will occur when government falls into the hands of lending institutions and moneyed incorporations."

~~ Thomas Jefferson, 1816

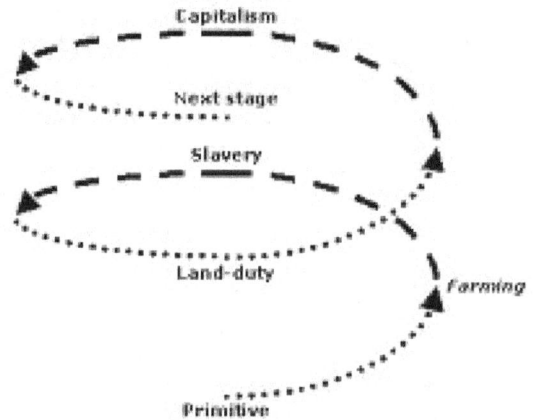

Fixing
the System

Gandhi's Wings: Occupy Wall Street and the Redistribution of Anxiety

We have reached a turning point. There is no more convincing people to play along in the "heads I win, tails you lose" game. We now plainly see that Atlas is strip mining our nation rather than carrying us on his shoulders of enterprise. The hero image of the business leader-provider is crumbling along with the core fabric of our society. Polls show that NYC citizens, Democrats and Republicans, and even Tea Party participants are all largely supportive of the protests. In Europe, many are ecstatic that America is finally objecting to the corruption at home that has been sliming the world for a long, long time. Etta James's "At Last" is being sung in the salons of Berlin and Paris.

Our secular religion of individualist economics is disintegrating in the face of a nightmarish experience. As the brilliant BBC documentary film series by Adam Curtis entitled "The Trap: What Happened to Our Idea of Freedom" illuminates, the every-man-for-himself concept of society and freedom creates a horrible void. The Horatio Alger myth has been refuted and shattered by reality. That old myth was attractive emotionally -- promising to resolve anxiety by teaching that if you put your head down and worked hard you could control your own fate.

But that lie was exposed when Wall Street blew itself up and millions lost their jobs, their homes, and their pensions through no fault of their own. The reckless financiers took us all down with them, and there was no way to insulate ourselves from their casino games and their manipulation of government. And the games just go on. The menace of high frequency trading is only the latest example of a system rigged against us. But we have begun to question a perverted notion of freedom, where the only thing we protect is the rights of the powerful to plunder the commons. We see that this "freedom" is so destructive that it is threatening the very integrity of our much-hallowed capital markets. What an irony! Compulsive greed cannot resist consuming its own monuments.

by Robert Johnson, Director of Economic Policy, Roosevelt Institute, NewDeal2.0

Systemic Problems Call For Systemic Solutions

Today, dire circumstances are pushing us into uncharted territory. Dire personal circumstances are pushing people into the streets to protest. Dire circumstances in the overall economy are pushing the Fed to assume unprecedented powers.

The severity or our recent financial crises made it clear that systemic problems now cry out for require systemic solutions. Our moment of reckoning has arrived and the birthing of Capitalism 3.0 is already upon us. There is a world of possibility awaiting us in the midst of our current economic crisis. The key to unlock this hidden potential is a new approach to "*The System.*" The current system–*The 3C System*–concentrates economic power in the hands of private, profit making institutions whose primary fiduciary responsibility is to provide a financial return to shareholders. That fiduciary responsibility trumps any other consideration, including the interests and needs of the larger society.

So *The System* ultimately doubles back upon itself and stares itself in the face, like an infinitely reflecting mirror of trust. Upon this trust has been constructed an entire edifice we call the global economy. It's an infinitely leveraged system built upon a foundation of debt that blows like sand in the wind. The debt based capital flows that are the lifeblood of our economy originate somehow, somewhere from within the inner sanctums of imposing temple-like structures in Washington, DC, huge banking towers that seem to touch the sky, and digital accounting entries that are as ephemeral as the 10 trillion dollars of wealth that simply evaporated during the recent liquidity crunch.

Today, there is righteous anger over the alleged fraud of bankers who were passing off toxic assets as sound investments; but this anger forgets about the long and distinguished tradition of swindling that has characterized the banking industry from its very inception. Student of economic history can cite a numerous examples of quick buck artists who chartered banks, issued bank notes and then absconded with the money, never redeeming the notes they issued. So the tradition continues with new tricks–financial innovations of increasing complexity invented at each new stage in the evolution of banking.

Which Way Do We Go?

What can we do to change the system? Regulatory reform has it's limitations because clever lawyers can always devise ways around laws and regulatory agencies tend to become captive of the sectors they are supposed to regulate. Laws enacted in earlier times are inadequate to deal with the scale and complexity of our current crisis. During crises there is a push towards increased oversight, but as crises subside and fade from public consciousness, the political forces are arrayed against regulation. Yes, President Obama put forth a tentative plan for increased oversight,

but the details and force behind it were lacking. The political power of Wall Street is was quickly mobilized to weaken what he proposed.[1]

Doing nothing is not an option. Without social innovation and change, we are all headed towards a future of continued instabilities, wild swings in confidence, eroding trust in the system and eventually the collapse of the dollar and the institutions upon which a stable currency is based. When these institutions start failing, their collapse will be seen as obvious–as obvious as the collapse of credit markets and the meltdown of the real estate market.

One thing is for sure. ... without some change is the system ... the larger system upon which we all depend will continue to weaken. This is inevitable ... the growth imperative of capitalism is on a collision course with the finite limits of the earth. Why? ... Read on ...

---

1 Chamber of Commerce Launches $100 Million Campaign to Protect Wall Street's Power at Our Expense: http://www.alternet.org/workplace/141031/

Irony Watch, Oakland edition, Updated

Apparently police used tear gas and batons to wreck Occupy Oakland's encampment this morning. Nothing very subtle about that. But it was the excuse from the mayor's office that caught my eye. According to the Oakland Tribune, a spokeswoman for the mayor, Karen Boyd, said Friday that the protesters had shown themselves incapable of self-governance. "As a collective, they cannot maintain the plaza in a safe condition," she said.

I haven't been to OccupyOakland, so can't speak to conditions. But at Wall Street, and in DC, and in Boston, I've seen people doing remarkable things, both outside and inside their camps. (Boston even has a library, with librarians from Boston Public). It's pretty sweet. But if the standard for successful governance is 'maintaining the plaza in a safe condition,' what does that say about the 1%? They've got a rapidly overheating planet, with an ocean 30% more acid than it used to be and the Arctic shedding sea ice. They've got endemic unemployment in almost every advanced economy, failing banks, and no answers to international conflicts beyond another round of drone flights. Maybe it's just me, but failing to "maintain the planet in a safe condition" seems like a worse charge. And if we need to be on the plazas over and over again to make that point, what choice really do we have?

- Bill McKibben - Author Activist

Economic Growth vs Limits of the Earth

In environmental circles there has long been a simmering conversation about the longer term ecological implications of an ever expanding economy. Suddenly the conversation is spilling over into the Occupy Wall Street's discussions of public and private debt. Without a clear consensus no solutions will be emerging in the corridors of power even with mounting evidence of systemic economic, social and environmental imbalances and instabilities. But when I consider that the population of the earth has tripled my lifetime, it really gives me pause.

ULTIMATELY THE VORACIOUS APPETITE OF AN IMBALANCED AND EVER EXPANDING ECONOMY WILL COLLIDE WITH THE FINITE LIMITS OF THE EARTH'S CARRYING CAPACITY. THIS SUGGESTS THE NEED FOR A FORM OF CAPITALISM 3.0 THAT VALUES NATURAL CAPITAL THAT MARKETS CURRENTLY DO NOT RECOGNIZE.

When we see things from this broader perspective, we understand the sense of urgency propelling the need for reform of "the system" that has created our problems. Carrying capacity is the maximum number of individuals of a specie that can be supported on a sustainable basis. When the population and its use of resources exceeds the earth's carrying capacity, both economic and environmental systems become unstable and imbalanced, as it uses up its finite supply of resources. If nothing is done to restore balances the population will eventually destroy both the economic and environmental systems that support it.

A Brief History of the Earth

This is a vignette often told by the late environmentalist, David Brower. It's his version of The history of the Planet Earth.

If we take the history of the planet earth, and condense it into just one week's time, beginning Sunday morning at midnight, consider these milestones:

- Life would not have appeared on the planet until midday on Tuesday.
- The great dinosaurs appeared on the earth at 4 P.M. on Saturday. They were offstage by 9 that evening.
- Homo-sapiens made their entrance at 30 seconds before midnight on Saturday.
- Agriculture began at 1 and 1/2 seconds before midnight.
- Jesus Christ made his entrance at 1/4 of a second before midnight.
- The industrial revolution took place at 1/40th of a second before midnight.
- World War I took place at 1/100th of a second before midnight.

Now consider what has happened in that last 1/100th of a second:
- The population of the Earth has increased threefold.
- The population of California has increased by a factor of 12.
- Humanity has used 4 times the amount of the earth's resources as were used in all previous history.

How long can we continue this pace of growth and still save our earth for future generations?

It is now midnight ... time to rethink!

There is an urgency in our economic and environmental predicament that begs for a solution. There is an instrument that is so powerful that it holds the possibility of trim tabbing the great ship of state headed full steam ahead towards a reckoning. *The great ship can only be turned quickly by a tiny trim tab on the rudder. This tiny instrument is money. By rethinking The Money Question we can change the direction of the great ship of state. Money itself is an instrument of transformation. Change takes time. Transformation takes place in an instant. Change creates upset. Transformation creates hope, vision and inspiration. We cannot have true change without transformation.*

There is ample basis for hope. Suddenly practitioners and visionaries from diverse fields are recognizing the need for systemic change. Discussions are taking place about new financial instruments, new markets, metrics and interoperability. Foundational to this thinking is a sense of urgency around the need for capital markets to more fully value environmental, social and other "externalities." The time is ripe to consolidate and catalyze these movements through one cohesive infrastructure that moderates the appetite of an ever examining economy by modernizing our concentrated, centralized and commercialized financial system.

THIS CAN BE ACCOMPLISHED THROUGH THE CREATION OF A PARALLEL NETWORK OF SMALLER, LOCALIZED, SPECIFIC PURPOSE, SOCIAL AND PUBLIC BANKS – ALL PART OF A "CREDIT COMMONS" THAT IS DEMOCRATIZED, DECENTRALIZED, DIGITIZED. THIS "CREDIT COMMONS" WILL BE ORGANIZED IN THE PUBLIC INTEREST OF THE MANY INSTEAD OF THE PRIVATE INTEREST OF A FEW. IT WILL ALSO INTEGRATE THE INTEREST OF THE PLANET INTO IT'S PROFIT MAXIMIZATION SCHEMA THROUGH TRIPLE BOTTOM LINE AND BLENDED VALUE ACCOUNTING PRINCIPLES.

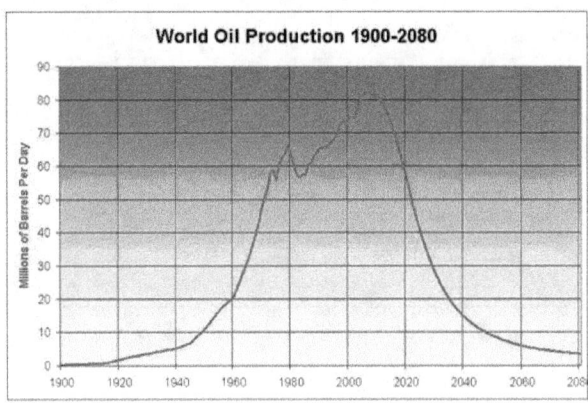

So Let's look at the future through the lens of realistic hope. Not some crispy creme wafer of hope, but the hard charging hope that is grounded in a hard cold assessment of what is possible. Let's explore the potential for systemic change based on what strategies of change have worked in the past. Lets imagine some of the kinds of public and Social Banks that will be created in this decentralized, democratized and digitized Social Banking System in Capitalism 3.0.

* * *

Last fall, our financial system stood on the brink of a collapse that threatened a depression. The crisis required our government to display wisdom, courage and decisiveness. Fortunately, the Federal Reserve and key economic officials in both the Bush and Obama administrations responded more than ably to the need.

They made mistakes, of course.
How could it have been otherwise when supposedly indestructible pillars of our economic structure were tumbling all around them? A meltdown, though, was avoided, with a gusher of federal money playing an essential role in the rescue.

The United States economy is now out of the emergency room and appears to be on a slow path to recovery. But enormous dosages of monetary medicine continue to be administered and, before long, we will need to deal with their side effects. For now, most of those effects are invisible and could indeed remain latent for a long time. Still, their threat may be as ominous as that posed by the financial crisis itself.

- Warren Buffett

NY Times, Op Ed, August 19, 2009, The Greenback Effect
http://www.nytimes.com/2009/08/19/opinion/19buffett.html

Quantum Economics

Imagine for a moment that you are Albert Einstein. At a moment of crisis in history, you've just had an intellectual breakthrough – a quantum leap forward in thinking that shatters the foundations of conventional thought. You have just advanced quantum physics with your Theory of Relativity. You believe that your theory will enable the development of the atom bomb, end the great war and unleash the most powerful force of energy the world has ever known. If you're right about your theory, the world will never be the same. Einstein was right about the Theory of Relativity and because of this, the consciousness of the world was transformed. Today we are at another crisis moment in history. Again, Einstein gives us the cue we need for an intellectual breakthrough about quantum economics - the basis of a more creative and conscious form of capitalism - *Capitalism 3.0*.

> NOT ALL THINGS THAT COUNT, CAN BE COUNTED ... AND NOT ALL THINGS THAT CAN BE COUNTED, COUNT.
>
> - ALBERT EINSTEIN

Contained in Einstein's simple insight is the philosophical foundation for a quantum leap forward in our thinking about the evolution of our money and banking system. This book expands on Einstein's simple insight with an idea that just might be the silver bullet economic experts have been searching for to awaken and revitalize our slumbering economy. The central trust of this book is that we are now dealing with the consequences of systemic problems that will require systemic solutions. Somehow we must find a way to measure and value things that our economic system ignores. Einstein's insight has implications for the banking system, our natural environment, government finances, Web based monetization and the entire landscape of business and social interaction. If Einstein is again right, his insight will enable us to create a new foundation the Credit Commons, a foundation upon which could be built an upgrade to our economic system, a sustainable and equitable economic system for the twenty-first century.

BREAK THE OLIGARCHY OF THE BIG BANKS

BIG BANKS, IT SEEMS, HAVE ONLY GAINED POLITICAL STRENGTH SINCE THE CRISIS BEGAN. AND THIS IS NOT SURPRISING. WITH THE FINANCIAL SYSTEM SO FRAGILE, THE DAMAGE THAT A MAJOR BANK FAILURE COULD CAUSE—LEHMAN WAS SMALL RELATIVE TO CITIGROUP OR BANK OF AMERICA—IS MUCH GREATER THAN IT WOULD BE DURING ORDINARY TIMES. THE BANKS HAVE BEEN EXPLOITING THIS FEAR AS THEY WRING FAVORABLE DEALS OUT OF WASHINGTON. ... AT THE ROOT OF THE BANKS' PROBLEMS ARE THE LARGE LOSSES THEY HAVE UNDOUBTEDLY TAKEN ON THEIR SECURITIES AND LOAN PORTFOLIOS. BUT THEY DON'T WANT TO RECOGNIZE THE FULL EXTENT OF THEIR LOSSES, BECAUSE THAT WOULD LIKELY EXPOSE THEM AS INSOLVENT. SO THEY TALK DOWN THE PROBLEM, AND ASK FOR HANDOUTS THAT AREN'T ENOUGH TO MAKE THEM HEALTHY (AGAIN, THEY CAN'T REVEAL THE SIZE OF THE HANDOUTS THAT WOULD BE NECESSARY FOR THAT), BUT ARE ENOUGH TO KEEP THEM UPRIGHT A LITTLE LONGER. THIS BEHAVIOR IS CORROSIVE: UNHEALTHY BANKS EITHER DON'T LEND (HOARDING MONEY TO SHORE UP RESERVES) OR THEY MAKE DESPERATE GAMBLES ON HIGH-RISK LOANS AND INVESTMENTS THAT COULD PAY OFF BIG, BUT PROBABLY WON'T PAY OFF AT ALL. IN EITHER CASE, THE ECONOMY SUFFERS FURTHER, AND AS IT DOES, BANK ASSETS THEMSELVES CONTINUE TO DETERIORATE—CREATING A HIGHLY DESTRUCTIVE VICIOUS CYCLE. ... TO BREAK THIS CYCLE, THE GOVERNMENT MUST FORCE THE BANKS TO ACKNOWLEDGE THE SCALE OF THEIR PROBLEMS. ... UNDER THESE CONDITIONS, CLEANING UP BANK BALANCE SHEETS IS IMPOSSIBLE.... BUT ONLY DECISIVE GOVERNMENT ACTION—EXPOSING THE FULL EXTENT OF THE FINANCIAL ROT AND RESTORING SOME SET OF BANKS TO PUBLICLY VERIFIABLE HEALTH—CAN CURE THE FINANCIAL SECTOR AS A WHOLE. ... BUT IN FACT, WHILE NECESSARY, IT IS INSUFFICIENT. THE SECOND PROBLEM THE U.S. FACES—THE POWER OF THE OLIGARCHY—IS JUST AS IMPORTANT AS THE IMMEDIATE CRISIS OF LENDING. AND THE ADVICE FROM THE IMF ON THIS FRONT WOULD AGAIN BE SIMPLE: BREAK THE OLIGARCHY. ... OVERSIZE INSTITUTIONS DISPROPORTIONATELY INFLUENCE PUBLIC POLICY; THE MAJOR BANKS WE HAVE TODAY DRAW MUCH OF THEIR POWER FROM BEING TOO BIG TO FAIL.
- SIMON JOHNSON, THE QUIET COUP, THE ATLANTIC, MAY 2009
   HTTP://WWW.THEATLANTIC.COM/DOC/200905/IMF-ADVICE

A Fundamental Power Shift

In the last 25 years there has been a fundamental shift in power taking place beneath the radar of public consciousness. 25 years ago "old money," represented by the major Wall Street banks, was the foundation of our banking system. But something significant has happened. In the interim, "new money" represented by technology firms like Apple, Google, Microsoft, Amazon, eBay, Cisco, and Facebook have created another power nexus to rival the Wall Street banks. During the peak of the financial crisis, Apple had more cash in its account than the U. S Treasury. Today, tech companies have a quarter of a trillion dollars in the bank, and their market caps are larger ... much larger than the big Wall Street banks. Taken collectively technology companies now have a more substantial and secure financial base than Wall Street banks and none of none of that money is leveraged. What are tech firms going to do with all the cash they have? The base of economic power has shifted from the financial firms of Wall Street to the technology firms of Silicon Valley.

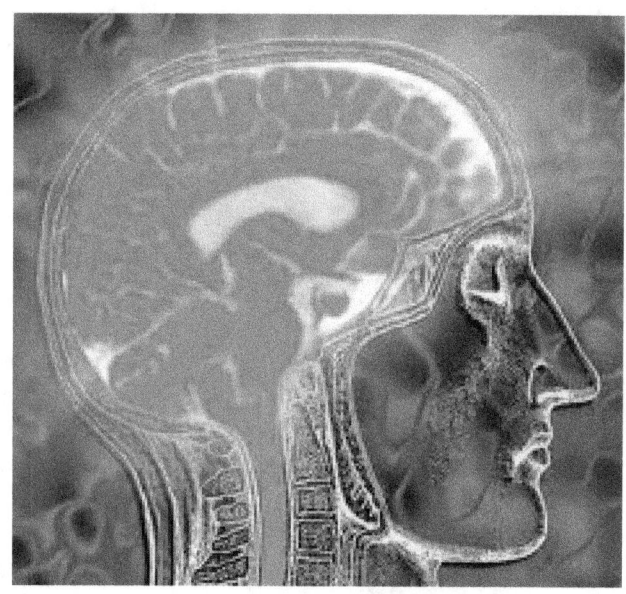

Connecting the Dots: Now let's connect the dots between this and other trends:
• social networking,
• digitization of finance,
• emerging mobile payment solutions
• new money's financial power,
• the technological prowess of new money companies,
• popular discontent with the old money and banking system embedded in the Occupy Wall Street movement.

Connecting the Dots

The world of new money has been progressing in fits and starts since the 1990s when "Cybercash" became the buzzword and startups with strange names like Flooz, Beenz, IcanBuy, Rocketcash, and Digicash, lead by visionary entrepreneurs, attracted serious venture capital, sometime millions of user for new kinds of money, in a matter of months.

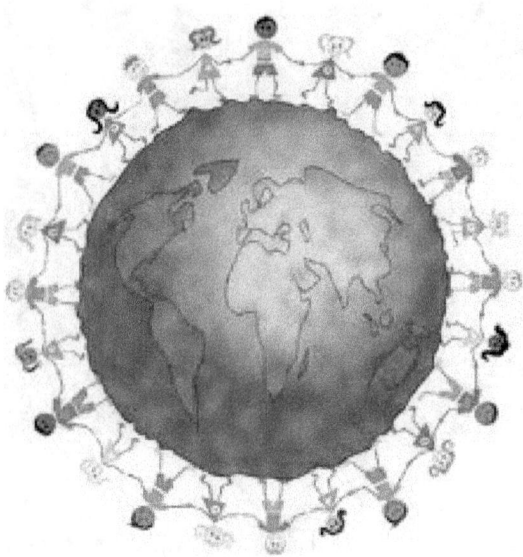

These startups were a decade ahead of their time. All except Paypal succumbed to the hard realities of the dot com crash, and ran out of capital. It was an ironic development for companies that were all about creating new forms of money. They were propelled by ideas like coupon money, smartcards, email money, giftcard money, points, rewards and lots of other variants. They were all unified by the belief that the nature of money itself was undergoing a fundamental shift.

Is it unrealistic to think that a parallel money and banking system could be overlaid on our existing money and banking system? Not at all, in fact the beginning stages of this are already unfolding. This new system can be much more efficient, much more equitable and much more empowering than our existing old money system if we embed it with design features that consciously integrate values of sustainability, equity and empowerment. These design features are all integrated into a cohesive and comprehensive vision for a new money and banking system called The Credit Commons. The Credit Commons is build on a platform called MaaSS. That stands for: money as a software service. Today most of our money is essentially digits created on computers. In essence, money has no essence today. So what's this Credit Commons all about.

A Big Idea ... Really Big!

The Credit Commons is a big idea ... really big. It's a natural evolution of the digital trends that started in the 1990's and have matured into more sophisticated platforms and programs. It's an idea whose time as come now that the flaws of the current financial system has moved from the mouths of experts into the common parlance of street protests. This idea is all about creating a complement to the system of "too big to fail banks." The Credit Commons is a new money and banking mechanisms for those who are disenchanted with our existing banking system. The Credit Commons is actually in its formative stages, but we don't realize it yet. The Credit Commons changes "the system" at the root level by democratizing the power to create money, just like the tech sector has already created platforms that democratize the power to create news, entertainment and other informational currencies. The Credit Commons can be created entirely itself through private enterprise and social action. The Credit Commons doesn't require any political debate or legislative reform.

Out of the Box Thinking: The Credit Commons reaches beyond tired economic thinking ... strait jackets of conventional theory and economic egotism. The Credit Commons represents a firm commitment to share our collective credit better, both with ourselves and with future generations. The Credit Commons is not anti-corporate. But it does recognize that the corporation that has a responsibility to the larger community, to the environment and to the future.

Merging Realism and Idealism: The Credit Commons is a realistic solution that invents our way out of our current economic malaise. The Credit Commons is a "pay it forward" economic innovation where we are consciously working together to build a better future. The Credit Commons is not only for economic activists. It's for investors who want to do well by doing good. It's for individuals, students and companies who want to reduce their debt. It's for anyone willing to take risks that offer tangible rewards both on the bottom line and in matters that go beyond the bottom line.

Transforming Anger into Action

The Credit Commons is a way to transform the frustration and raw anger into purposeful action. People all over are feeling anger about a system they perceive to be unfair. The Credit Commons is a vehicle for pooling our capital and our anger into channels that can empower all of us. The Credit Commons integrates social banking, digital e-commerce and venture philanthropy.

A Collaborative and Sustainable Economy: The Credit Commons doesn't look for state help or handouts from public coffers. It looks to builds mutual self help into the banking system ... Social Bank to Social Bank ... neighbor to neighbor ... stranger to stranger ... and connection through a network of trust that extends from the collective store of trust within each of the enterprises, individuals and institutions that come together to build this parallel money and banking system. The Credit Commons is are embedded with values of sustainability, efficiency, equity and democracy.

Sanctioned by People and Private Enterprise Instead of by Government: The Credit Commons isn't sanctioned by any government. But it does represent the best ideals of good government. Political support for the Credit Commons will ultimately be inevitable because no politician that cares for or listens to their constituents will dare to oppose it. The Credit Commons won't pad the pockets of politicians with campaign contributions, but it will help fill government coffers with supplemental revenues generated by the commerce it stimulates. The Credit Commons is both private enterprise and a social enterprise ... It's a public venture, and a collective adventure into what our imagination can produce.

Rewriting the Code of The Operating System for the Global Economy

The Credit Commons all about writing a new code for the global operating system. It's a Common Cents Code that imbues the new system with deeper values ... values of sustainability, economic justice, peace, educational improvement and democracy.

Representing the 99%: The Credit Commons is designed to represent the economic rights and interests of the 99%. The Credit Commons is an affirmation of the economic power we already have. Economic power that flows from out choice about how we use our money. ... how we spend it ... invest it .... deposit it ... lend it. The Credit Commons represents multi-constituencies, diverse communities and multi-disciplinary solutions.

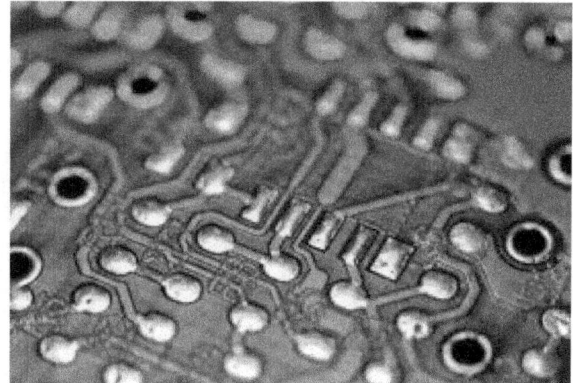

A MaaSS Movement: The Credit Commons is built upon a MaaSS Movement - with Money as a Software Service. The Credit Commons extends and expands the Occupy Movement that is now unfolding. It's the natural evolution of the questions that are now being asked in the protests all across the country. As trust erodes in our existing money and banking system, that trust is can be transferred to a new system the outlines of which are emerging. The Credit Commons constitutes a paradigm shift in our thinking about the most powerful tool ever created by humans–money.

Systemic Solutions to Systemic Problems: Are there systemic solutions to the problems that people have taken to the street to protest? Could we achieve unprecedented levels of collaboration to build a Credit Commons and a new MaaSS Can be create a parallel money platform that sees money in entirely new digital form of social media ... disrupting money and banking systems ... transforming them into a system that is more efficient, more equitable and more empowering than old money systems.

Old Money vs New Money

An unrecognized trend is already moving us towards towards privately created new money... None of these entities creating private money are currently thought of as banks, but in point of fact they are performing banking functions. More and more money money substitutes are being created not by banks, but rather by other private entities. .... retailers ... airlines ... private communities. We call this new money things like points, rewards, coupons, gift certificates, airline miles, community currencies. Did you know that one of the largest circulating currencies in the world today is airline miles. 17 trillion airline miles are in circulation with a market value of between $500 million and $1 trillion. All this new money is create by private non bank institutions, and gifted into circulation rather than created as debt. This is a noteworthy trend. Can this be extended and expanded? First let's look at the problems we face.

Problems Addressed: There are several problems being addressed simultaneously.

• First it addressing an endemic problem in our economy ... stimulating demand for idle capacity ... filling empty seats ... bringing benefits to businesses that exceed their costs in purchasing their new Moneeey from the Credit Commons.

• Second it's enabling partners to make a lot of money because it's addressing the problems with inefficient flows of capital in our economy. Commercial banks have cut back on lending because economic conditions don't suggest that there are a lot of good uses for their capital. They were traumatized by the financial crisis of 2007=8 .. They don't want to have huge write offs on loans ... So money isn't flowing ... that's what economic downturns are all about ... But this system puts more money into the economy and targets that new money to very specific uses ... because those uses of New Moneeey can be embedded right in the tags of the money itself.

• Third it address a huge social problem ... it's proving new and sustainable sources of capital to organizations that are now starved for capital ... It is transferring some of the money creation power, heretofore exclusively the domain of banks, transferring this power to non banks ...

• Fourth and finally it's enabling non banks to achieve financial leverage their operations.

Historical Context

The nature of money has been evolving for millennia ... There as a time when people used sheep as money ... then stones ... then coins ... then paper money ... then electronic notations ... Today most of what we think of as money is nothing more than digits exchanged on computers. Today over $4 trillion dollars of these digits are exchanged on global currency markets every day ... you heard that right 4 trillion are exchanged every day on global currency markets.

An Oligarchy of Private Banks: All this money has been created by an oligopoly of private profit making institutions we call banks. All these banks are part of centralized banking systems. In the United States they are part of the Federal Reserve System. Other countries have centralized banking systems. But a fundamental power shift has taken place in our economy ... largely unnoticed. Economic power has shifted from private banks to technology companies.

A Dangerously Leveraged System: All these banks are highly leveraged ... They have levels of debt that constantly scare financial markets and lead to periodic panics. Were the stock market to tank, again, several major banks would be in trouble ... our entire financial system would be in trouble should any one of them approach insolvency. It's a fundamentally flawed system. But to change the system we first have to understand how the system works.

LEVERAGE

'Give me a place to stand, and I will move the Earth.' - Archimedes

System Design Considerations

The structure of any new *Money and Banking System* must address the following:

- How can we stabilize our economy?
- How can we better balance our priorities?
- How can we make our economy more equitable?
- How can we reduce default rates of distressed borrowers?
- How can we promote needs over greed?
- How can we reduce government borrowing?
- How can we empower groups and citizens working for the public interest?
- How can we find the money to improve our educational system and universities?
- How can we provide capital for renewable energy companies and consumers?
- How can we provide incentives for people to reduce their carbon footprint?
- How can we protect, preserve and promote the natural environment?
- How can we enable non profit groups and foundations to expand their impact?
- How can we enable philanthropists to leverage their giving in charitable dollars?
- How can we stimulate investment is social enterprises and social innovation?
- How can we enable students to get an education without going deeply into debt?
- How can we revitalize our community spirit?
- How can we renew our commitment to the common good?
- How can we stimulate a sustainable economic recovery?
- How can we improve the quality of health care for all?
- How can small businesses find the capital they need to thrive?
- How can we stimulate new waves of wealth creation?
- How can we promote social and economic justice?
- How can we provide essential services for the elderly, infirm and poor?
- How can we provide incentives for people to adopt preventive health measures?
- How can we get people to improve their nutrition and get more exercise?
- How can we provide greater compensation for teachers and creative artists?
- How can we spur volunteerism and greater sharing of resources?
- How can we maintain our stature in the world?

Seeing a Better Future Through 3D Glasses

Nothing will change until we come up with a better solution to the issue of who has the power in our society to create money. There is a better way. If we extend the power to create money to other institutions in society, it will be possible

to break the bonds of this form of debt slavery. This will not be easy. Bankers not only have economic power, but they also have the political power to influence public policy and perpetuate the status quo. Ultimately, America itself suffers most in this system. America has become beholden to foreign investors who hold trillions of dollars of U.S. Treasuries.

The question about who creates money can be addressed in one of three ways. The power to create money can be vested with the private sector, the public sector or the social sector. The current answer relies exclusively on the first option. In *3C Capitalism*, the power to create money is given to an oligarchy of private commercial banks including the Federal Reserve Bank. But there is a better way: the 3D form of Capitalism 3.0 where the power to create money is *d e c e n t r a l i z e d, d e m o c r a t i z e d a n d d i g i t i z e d.*

IN THE 3D FORM OF CAPITALISM 3.0, THE PUBLIC SECTOR, AND THE SOCIAL SECTOR WILL ALSO BE INVITED TO THE BANKING AND INVESTMENT BANKING PARTY, THROUGH THE CREDIT COMMONS.

"The Movement" is now opening debate over these issues. Technology now provides us with intriguing possibilities for new ways to create and exchange money. We no longer need to give banks a complete monopoly over the creation of money. Other institutions with an integrated set of social, ecological and financial motivations can be empowered to create a new form of money to complement and stabilize the existing money supply. This simple innovation can redress the imbalances of the current system. We need not act out of vengefulness or fear, but we do need to act.

Retrofitting the System with a Credit Commons

Let's face reality … we're not going to bring down the system … nor do we want to. But we can retrofit the existing money and banking system so that it can both be more just and more resilient in the face of future tremors … which surely are coming. Such a retrofit involves the creation of a parallel layer that will ameliorate some of the inequities and inefficiencies of the current system. With the advent of technological solutions like cybercash, digital wallets, mobile payments, social networks and NFC chips. we're entering a new frontier in money systems.

> "WE ARE IN UNCHARTED TERRITORY IN THIS CRISIS."
> - ECONOMIST, JOSEPH STIGLITZ

At the root level, we need to look at the motivations that are built into the DNA of our current economic system, especially the composition and character of the money and markets that are the lifeblood of our economy. At the most fundamental level, the root cause of our financial crisis is that our economic system is propelled by a dynamic of increasing imbalances between those who create wealth and those who create value for our society. Those with financial power and credibility tend to have greater access to debt and equity capital markets than those without such credibility and power. As a result, they are able to enhance their economic stature by creating wealth through increasingly exotic and highly leveraged financial instruments. Are these wizards creating value to society? While this happens, the economic situation of those at the bottom of the economic ladder is diminished as they struggle to survive–digging themselves deeper and deeper into a mountain of debt until many end up in default. Numerous studies have documented how the dynamics of our economic system tend to exacerbate economic inequalities. The line of demarcation between the haves and have nots in our society is often access to credit. The playing field can be leveled with a new answer in the form of the Credit Commons and a *3D Form of Capitalism 3.0* . The Credit Commons is a carefully considered and innovative plan to awaken the economy by democratizing the power to create money in an advanced form of Capitalism 3.0.

This isn't a new idea. As far back as revolutionary days, people like Thomas Jefferson spoke of the need for democratizing the powers that had been delegated to banks.

> # THE ISSUING POWER SHOULD BE TAKEN FROM THE BANKS AND RESTORED TO THE PEOPLE TO WHOM IT PROPERLY BELONGS.
>
> ## - THOMAS JEFFERSON

The Credit Commons will use technology to take back some of that power and delegate it to social banks that can provide supplemental capital and credit to businesses, non profits, schools, universities social entrepreneurs – any entity that needs capital to accomplish something that is in society's long term interest. Capitalism 3.0 will help promote green lifestyles, catalyze a new wave of wealth creation, empower the social economy, promote the common good and introduce economic justice into the DNA of the market based economy. In a single bold stroke, The Credit Commons will enable us to seize control of our financial future while creating societal scale financial incentives for socially, economically and environmentally sustainable behavior.

There are good reasons why Wall Street bankers should be open to calls for reform. Bankers know that the system has grown increasingly unstable? They also know that our banking system is so highly leveraged, it only takes a small number of borrowers defaulting on their loans or mortgages to destabilize the system. The bankers' fundamental challenge is to reduce the risk of defaults by those most vulnerable to an economic downturn. To stabilize the system, they must find a way to reduce the level of risk of defaults. A parallel network of Social Banks issuing a "social currency" can constitute a systemic safety net that will not only make the banking system more stable, but will also help those most in need without incurring the governmental debt associated with welfare, or bank bailouts. Banks, rather than resisting change, can become partners building a more modernized banking system– The Credit Commons–democratized, decentralized and digitized. The 3D form of Capitalism 3.0 sees the world through a different lens–more modern perspective–a perspective of public purpose rather than private interest. This 3D Solution won't be a substitute for The 3C System, but rather a complement. It will operate in parallel to the existing 3C banking and money system. The Credit Commons will help make Capitalism 3.0 real. It will help make our overall economy more stable, balanced and equitable.

3D Capitalism 3.0 will not only empower Main Street. It will also empower foundations, universities, non-profits, community groups, small businesses, social enterprises and other institutions vital to the overall health of society. It will embolden them by granting them the power to create money. THE NEED FOR THIS SYSTEM GROWS OUT OF THE FACT THAT THE GROUPS AND PEOPLE WHO ARE IN THE BEST POSITION TO ADVANCE OUR COMMON INTERESTS ARE, LARGELY, STARVED OF THE CAPITAL THEY NEED TO ADVANCE THEIR MISSION. In essence we have a highly inefficient financial infrastructure to support the private sector, and an even more inefficient system to support the environment, education, research, the arts, communities, equity and everything else we value in society. These are fundamental and ultimately fatal flaws of a system desperately in need of modernization.

"We the people" already have all the power we need to establish new social and community based public and Social Banks that can create money using the Internet and other digital tools just like commercial banks today create money when they make loans.

The challenge that awaits us is essentially extending the meaning of democracy to the economic realm, by democratizing the power to create money. The use of social dollars will be entirely voluntary. Anyone using social dollars will be doing so as an affirmation of values and principles that support sustainability, financial stability and economic justice.

Capitalism 3.0 is a very big idea, but it's not wild or unrealistic. Indeed, it's a necessary adaptation of our financial system to the needs of a society that must now give credence to broader issues that will affect all of us for generations to come. We don't have to accept an antiquated answer to *The Money Question*. We don't have to accept financial crises and rising public and private debts that threaten America's future. We don't have to accept banking bailouts, toxic assets and all the rest that goes with the current system. This debate goes to the heart of the American character. Do we want to continue to feed the rapacious appetite of Wall Street, or do we want to level the playing field and empower the citizens of Main Street? The choice is ours.

What is the Credit Commons?

The mechanics of the Credit Commons are explained more fully in a companion book, **Common Cents: New Money vs Old Money and the Next American Revolution.** But in summary form:

★ The Credit Commons is a democratic retrofit to The Federal Reserve System.

★ The Credit Commons is a complementary money and banking system, designed to be layered upon the existing money and banking system.

★ Because it is entirely digital and organized in the common interest, the Credit Commons can be more stable, more secure and more sustainable than the existing money system which is propelled entirely by self interest.

★ The Credit Commons doesn't seek change through political legislation or reform. It changes the system at the root level itself through private enterprise and social action.

★ The Credit Commons represents multi-constituencies, diverse communities and multi-disciplinary solutions.

★ The Credit Commons reaches beyond tired economic thinking ... strait jackets of conventional theory and economic egotism.

★ The Credit Commons represents a firm commitment to better share our resources, both with ourselves and with future generations.

- ★ The Credit Commons is a "pay it forward" economic innovation where we are consciously working together to build a better future.

- ★ The Credit Commons is not an idealistic solution. It is a realistic solution that invents our way out of our current economic malaise.

- ★ The Credit Commons is a way to mainstream the frustration people all over are feeling about a system they perceive to be unfair.

- ★ The Credit Commons integrates social banking, digital e-commerce and venture philanthropy.

- ★ The Credit Commons is a vehicle for pooling our capital in ways that empower all of us.

- ★ The Credit Commons is not only for economic activists. It's for investors who want to do well by doing good. It's for executives who want to reduce their debt loads. It's for anyone willing to take risks that offer tangible rewards both on the bottom line and in matters that go beyond the bottom line.

- ★ The Credit Commons doesn't look for state help or handouts from public coffers. It looks to mutual self help ... neighbor to neighbor ... stranger to stranger ... and connection through a network of trust that extends from the collective store of trust within each of the enterprises, individuals and institutions that come together to build this parallel money and banking system.

- ★ The Credit Commons isn't sanctioned by any government. But it does represent the best ideals of good government. Political support for the Credit Commons will be inevitable because no politician that cares for or listens to their constituents will dare to oppose it.

- ★ The Credit Commons won't pad the pockets of politicians with campaign contributions, but it will help fill government coffers.

- ★ The Credit Commons will be a substantial source of new income for government, while simultaneously stimulating commerce with more capital flowing through channels of commerce ....

★ The Credit Commons channels capital more efficiently towards what is working incorporating community feedback loops to measure and monetize what markets currently ignore.

★ The Credit Commons is both private enterprise and a social enterprise ... It's a public venture, and a collective adventure into what our imagination can produce.

★ The Credit Commons is a new code of Common Cents for the global operating system. It's a code that imbues the new system with deeper values ... values of sustainability, economic justice, peace, educational improvement and democracy.

★ The Credit Commons is not designed to replace the Federal Reserve, but rather complement it and represent the rights and interest of the 99%.

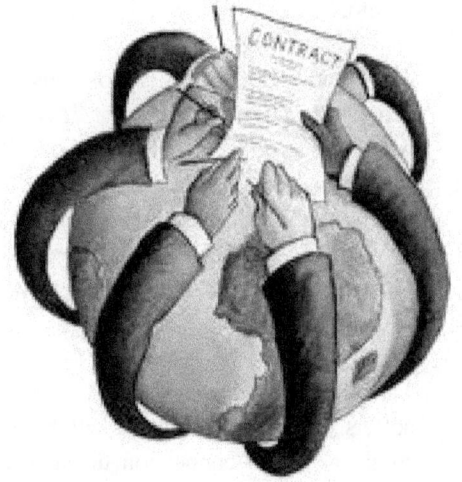

★ The Credit Commons is an affirmation of the economic power we already have. Economic power that flows from out choice about how we use our money. ... use in the sense of spend it ... invest it .... deposit it ... lend it.

★ The Credit Commons is are embedded with values of sustainability, efficiency, equity and democracy.

★ The Credit Commons is not anti-corporate. But it does view the corporation that has a responsibility to the larger community and environment.

★ The Credit Commons is an institutional approach to move beyond our myopic preoccupation with the bottom line and the unquestioned value of profit.

★ The Credit Commons is a sophisticated software platform that enables many different values to become embedded in the way we create, uses, share and exchange our money.

★ The Credit Commons enables many different currencies to circulate through the same money system .... call them what you will iBucks, Social Dollars, Bear Bucks ... Gator Dollars ... Crimson Cash ... all of these currencies will be created by Social Banks working as part of the Credit Commons.

★ The Credit Commons will build trust in the system as the sum of the accumulated trust that all the entities that are part of the system bring to it. The partners will be institutions with a store of legitimacy or community support ... universities.

★ Each of these institutions will embed in their use of money the values that honor their mission.

★ The Credit Commons will tap the best minds available to program the Common Cents Code of the software platform ... enabling a MaaSS Movement where Money is a Software Service ... that serves the interest of all of us.

★ All these currencies will have dual lives ... they will circulate within the communities that issue them ... and can be redeemed by those communities ... and also they will interact with each other in the larger system ... tradable ... exchangeable ... always their value fluctuation according to their exchange rate on the larger exchange.

★ The Credit Commons is not about penny ante stuff. The Credit Commons intends to tap into the 4 trillion dollars that change hands every day on global currency exchanges.

★ The Credit Commons intends to divert some of the speculative activity of that f that 4 trillion dollar marketplace towards new currency markets represent broader interests.

★ The Credit Commons will incorporate the idea of a Robin Hood Tax that assesses a transactional commission on all exchanges and passes part of that income onto worthy projects that the community at large validates.

* The Credit Commons will incorporate a negative interest rates on funds that sit idle so that the velocity of money flowing through the system will increase.

* The Credit Commons will use sophisticated metrics to adjust levers in real time to insure that inflation is kept under control.

* The Credit Commons will incorporate the most sophisticated encryption technology to guard against fraud and abuse.

* The Credit Commons will help breaks the oligarchy of the big banks by democratizing the power to create money.

* The Credit Commons requires no legislation. It's a private social enterprise. Regulatory approvals will be necessary but no legislation need to create it.

* The Credit Commons will cut out the middleman in many financial transactions. A platform that enables mutual credit relationships directly between companies will enable businesses to borrow directly from each other rather than having to cut in the banks with their fees and interest rates.

* The Credit Commons will enable everybody to set up a digital wallet. In that digital wallet they can store many different kinds of currencies.

* Does this all sound too good to be true ... Read on to find out why it's all possible.

Mechanics of the Credit Commons System

The Credit Commons is a social enterprise that bridges the divide between philanthropy and business enterprise. It is an ecosystem that includes retailers, major banks, credit card companies, social networks, search engines, universities, foundations and other institutions with a sufficient store of legitimacy to establish the trust necessary to scale the entire system.

1. All forms of new Moneeey are digital and are initially created by the Credit Commons. Because the Credit Commons is a non profit, any Moneeey it creates is exempt from SEC regulation.

2. Moneeey partners (businesses, nonprofits and government agencies) must be certified as "social banks" by the Credit Commons. The certification process is rigorous. It requires the submission and approval of a Moneeey Plan that specifies:
• the uses of their Moneeey,
• size of their customer, client or community base,
• their redemption mechanisms (if any),
• financial wherewithal,
• the characteristics of the Moneeey they will use including currency name, appearance, premium services, tags, geographic restrictions, expiration dates, etc.

3. Once certified, "social banks" are plugged into the MaaSS (Money as a Software Service) platform. This cloud based system enables them to:
• design their own individually branded forms of Moneeey,
• establish their digital vault to hold their reserves of Moneeey,
• sign up customers and create their digital wallets,
• account for all transactions in new Moneeey,
• issue new Moneeey to their constituents, customers, clients or communities.
• Moneeey Purchases: Social Banks purchase new Moneeey from the Credit Commons at a floating "discount rate," (ie. twenty cents on the dollar) determined by an algorithm that incorporates:
• Donations: Donors make tax deductible contributions to the Credit Commons.

• Advertising and Marketing: Moneeey partners and Social Banks pay Moneeey, Inc. or the Credit Commons for advertising and premium services such as customization and the ability to embed links, photos or videos in new Moneeey.

5. New Moneeey is issued into circulation in two ways:
• Social Banks and Moneeey partners gift it into circulation using it to structure granular coupons, gift cards or discounting programs and/or design incentives for socially, environmentally, economically or educationally beneficial activity.
• The Credit Commons awards grants to nonprofits, businesses or individuals that are members of the Credit Commons. These grants are awarded like prizes to those that are exemplary or achieve certain goals.

6. Moneeey is exchanged in commerce, circulating parallel to cash and used primarily to obtain discounts or rewards while shopping. All transactions in Moneeey are accounted for using the MaaSS Moneeey Movement software platform. Purchases can be made with the convenience of normal transactions using credit cards, computers or mobile devices.

7. Moneeey is withdrawn from circulation in three ways:
• Moneeey Inc. charges a demurrage fee (negative interest rate) for idle funds held in members' digital wallet. This creates an incentive for members to use their Moneeey or lose it, thus increasing the velocity of Moneeey flow.
• Moneeey Inc. assesses a transactional commission on all exchanges in the Moneeey system.
• Moneeey Inc. retires Moneeey from circulation after it has done sufficient work (ie. X number of exchanges) or after it has reached its expiration date.
• legal status and other corporate characteristics,
• market conditions,
• community feedback.

8. Cash Out: Moneeey Inc. now has new Moneeey in its digital vault and the Credit Commons has cash in its vault. Moneeey Inc. sells their Moneeey to the Credit Commons for cash. Moneeey Inc. applies this cash to: • Pay taxes,
• Pay operational expenses,
• Retained earnings,
• Sharing with members of the system.

9. Cash Bonuses to Members: Members using new Moneeey in commerce can, in effect, win a bonus when Moneeey they have acquired in a transaction has done sufficient work (x number of exchanges) to be withdrawn from circulation and redeemed for cash. Thus some members also are able to periodically "cash out" their new Moneeey from the system, but the timing and amount of "cash out" is determined algorithmically by the Credit Commons depending on the market conditions.

10. This innovative system creates a win-win-win proposition where:
• consumers both receive discounts while shopping and have the added incentive of receiving a cash bonus for using new Moneeey,
• businesses can create their own branded, media rich currencies and use them to stimulate business through flexible, real-time adjustable discounting programs,
• nonprofits, foundations, schools, universities and businesses gain access to new and sustainable sources of capital while leveraging their scarce capital.

The Credit Commons Ecosystem

The Credit Commons Ecosystem is a network of businesses and retailers who agree to issue or redeem individually branded currencies, created by social banks that have been certified by the Credit Commons. Once certified, these social banks can create money and issue it into circulation to their customers, clients, communities and constituencies. Let's call these currencies together "social dollars." Social Dollars can be used in commerce in partial or complete payment for goods and services. Online retailers would display "Credit Commons" buttons on their Website or on  shelves in stores to indicate they are part of *The Social Dollar Retail Network*. Just as many local merchants have embraced the alternative currencies as a way to show their support for the community, major retailers, service providers and banks will soon learn the branding value of participating in this socially innovative system.

WITH SUSTAINABLE INCOME SOURCES AND ACCESS TO CAPITAL MARKETS, SOCIAL ENTREPRENEURS AND NON PROFITS WILL NO LONGER BE SEEN AS BEGGARS AND OUTCASTS, BUT RATHER A VITAL PLAYERS IN SOCIETY, WHO HAVE THE RESOURCES THEY NEED TO DEVELOP AND SCALE PROGRAMS OF REAL IMPACT.

Why would they want to participate? The answer is simple. It's in their self interest. Clearly there are good business reasons why major corporate brands will find it in their self interest to support a community based currency like social dollars. Corporations routinely spend hundreds of billions of dollars building brand awareness and brand loyalty through promotional programs. This is not just charity. It's good business, because it helps create shareholder value by creating a positive brand image. Because of the social benefit to both companies and consumers, the size of the Social Dollar Retail Network is likely to grow with viral speed. One can easily imagine the use of social dollars through a Social Credit Card tracking system:

- Supermarket chains displaying small signs next to items on store shelves indicating the price of an item with and without the Social Credit Card, not unlike they now show what the price is if the consumer uses their Club Card.
- Online retailers displaying a small button that indicates that they are members of The Social Dollar Retail Network.
- Advertisers use their affiliation with The Social Dollar Retail Network in their brand building campaigns.

- eBay lets buyers and sellers use social dollars for partial payment, with sellers indicating what percentage of the agreed upon price they will accept in social dollars.
- New online exchanges and auction sites are formed to enable barter using Social Dollars as a medium of exchange.
- Credit card companies offer social dollars whenever shoppers use their card.
- Travel companies use social dollars as part of promotional campaigns.
- Municipal governments offer tax incentives for people who use social dollars.
- Schools and universities offer meal discounts to students who use social dollars.
- Churches accept donations in social dollars and pass them onto beneficiaries of their outreach programs.
- Non profits use social dollars to compensate volunteers.
- Doctors use social dollars to encourage their patients to adopt healthy lifestyles, take their medicine or participate in community health building activities.

Many of these forms of activity are currently not recognized or undervalued by our existing market-based economy. The introduction of social dollars will stimulating the overall economy and inject liquidity into the system by valuing what that was previously undervalued and attaching a more accurate value to it. The challenge of accurately measuring economic activity was described by Clifford Cobb, Ted Halstead, and Jonathan Rowe in their prescient article: *If the GDP is Up, Why is America Down? The Atlantic*, October 1995. Here is a quote from that pathbreaking article.

Is the GDP an Accurate Measure of Economic Activity?

The GDP is simply a gross measure of market activity, of money changing hands. It makes no distinction whatsoever between the desirable and the undesirable, or costs and gain. On

top of that, it looks only at the portion of reality that economists choose to acknowledge--the part involved in monetary transactions. The crucial economic functions performed in the household and volunteer sectors go entirely unreckoned. As a result the GDP not only masks the breakdown of the social structure and the natural habitat upon which the economy--and life itself-- ultimately depend; worse, it actually portrays such breakdown as economic gain.

- Clifford Cobb, Ted Halstead, and Jonathan Rowe

Private and Complementary Currencies

Today there are thousands of forms of money, though we call them names like rewards, points, airline miles, coupons, smartcards, gift cards, complementary, alternative and community currencies. Most of these forms of money exist as islands unto themselves. With the arrival of the digital age, it is now technologically feasible to create an entirely digital and parallel money system where all these forms of money can be exchanged against each other and against dollars.

Wherever there is trust, money can be created, if the proper mechanisms for transfer and exchange are developed. Although our government has vested banks with exclusive authority to create the official government currency, unofficial "social" currencies can be created by anyone that has a network of trust established in which that currency is generally accepted as a medium of exchange. Now combine this with all the potentialities that exist in the electronic age, the age of the Internet and suddenly you have the essential elements of an idea of transformative power: creating interoperability between government, private, local and complementary currencies:

This parallel money and banking platform can also serve as a medium of exchange in Web based social networks and communities throughout our society. Will this open up even more possibilities? I believe so. When we vest social networks, communities, schools, universities, churches, environmental organizations and other groups in the social sector economy with the ability to create money as social dollars, it will result in a fundamental power shift that will have a profoundly beneficial effect on our society. It will unleash an explosion of creative energy. It will revitalize the social sector. It will start to bring real and constructive progress towards the solution of many of our most vexing and intractable social problems.

This parallel money system is both achievable and of transformative power. This system of public and Social Banks will be supported and embraced by a wide array of groups, corporate marketers, government agencies, cultural and civic groups. Why? Simple economics. The system is giving them power ... the power to create money. Their charge is create economic incentives for behavior that is in the common interests instead of private gain. With is as a guiding ethic, suddenly you have all kinds of people and groups who are willing to accept social dollars as a medium of exchange because they have trust in the groups that are creating the money, trust in the entity that is managing The System and trust the people who are using it. Altogether it is an expanding network of trust.

Imagine all the things that can be encouraged with the use of social dollars. Incentives can be created for an infinite array good ideas that benefit society at large:

• Green building practices
• Green lifestyles
• Reducing climate change
• Community building
• Creative expression
• Educational and learning incentives
• Strengthening of religious and spiritual connections
• Support for underprivileged people
• Diversity
• Peace initiatives
• Socially responsible investing
• Social marketing
• Encouraging people to shop their values
• Startup of social enterprises
• Charitable giving

The potential benefits of this rethinking of the nature of money will be profound. Money is arguably the most powerful motivation tool ever created. Using this social currency it will be possible to create and implement societal scale incentives for companies and individuals to adopt the kinds of lifestyle changes that are required for us to address the climate change crisis in a real way.

This social currency has the potential to transform the world of philanthropy. It will open up new and sustainable income sources to foundations, universities, arts and civic groups and virtually any entity that is acting in the public interest. By introducing the power of financial leverage to the DNA of the social economy and entire sector of the economy will be empowered in a way that is simply not possible under the current system. Suddenly we will see all kinds of creative solutions emerging from an empowered sector that now has adequate capital resources to scale their ideas quickly and efficiently.

The net effect of this system will be to stabilize our entire financial system. The circulating social dollars will act as a flywheel to mitigate the excesses of the current system. Foundations acting as Social Banks will be empowered to issue social dollars to help out those in need. It will in effect be a economic safety net that doesn't place a drag on the federal budget or incur all the encumbrances of a governmental bureaucracy.

Clearly the implementation of this system will require an unprecedented level of collaboration between private sector, the social sector and government. Some form of governmental oversight may be required to insure the soundness of the system, or perhaps it could be administered by a community based oversight panel without governmental regulation. Retailers will agree to accept social dollars in partial payment of most transactions. Banks will agree to accept social dollars in return for reduced interest rates for qualifying entities and individuals. An infrastructure will be created for the accounting and exchange if social dollars, most probably through existing bank, ATM, credit card and computer networks. On eBay social dollars are accepted in partial payment in transactions.

Is it really so farfetched to assume that major corporations and retailers will participate in such a program? Not really. It is in the self interest of banks and other corporate interests to undertake efforts to stabilize the financial system. It's also in their self interest to generate goodwill and positive brand awareness for their firms. Today major corporations invest hundreds of millions of dollars in rewards programs that accomplish essentially the same purpose. Take a quick look at the astounding sums that some of these companies currently spend polishing their brand image. In 2007 Verizon spent $408 million on marketing and advertising. At&T spent $364 million. IBM spent $194 million. Citigroup spent $149 million. Bank of America - $89 million. Staples spent $116 million. Microsoft - $171 million. Apple Computer - $91 million. Visa - $62 million. Mastercard - $47 million. The list goes on an on. Will these companies be interested in using some of this money to gain the goodwill that will accrue to them by participating in a program that encourages behavior that is for the greater good of society?

Some implicit built-in mechanisms in money systems have social implications. ... All the money we have is debt-generated -- someone goes to a bank and makes a loan. This pits people against each other, collectively. Competition is built into The System. Greed and the breakdown of community that everybody is complaining about correlate with the use of competitive money systems.

- Bernard Lietaer, Author, "The Future of Money"

Organizing for Change

What awaits us is a challenge of good old fashioned entrepreneurial spirit combined with community organizing ... that is ... building a network of partnerships and people who want to make the existing system more efficient, more equitable and more empowering ... working towards change in our banking system–building a new and more modernized money and banking structure. Are there enough people who will be willing to embrace a better solution to the monopolistic, infinitely leveraged, unstable, concentrated, centralized commercialized banking system we have now? The foundations of this community already exist and are getting support from high places–even White House.

REMEMBER THAT WHOLE THING ABOUT FIXING OUR FINANCIAL SYSTEM?

"Everybody understands," Geithner said on This Week, "that we cannot have our financial system go back to the practices that brought this economy to the brink of collapse." It's true, we all understand it. The problem is, the system has already gone back. Risky derivatives are traded again, bonuses disconnected from performance are being handed out again, bank lobbyists are spending tens of millions to undermine necessary regulatory reforms again. The only real long-term solution is for the government to ensure that there are no financial institutions too big to fail anymore, so that if they continue to act irresponsibly, then they are just allowed to fail. That's capitalism, remember? The creative-destruction consequences of a free-enterprise system that all these bonus-loving bankers love to extol. If we're really going to protect taxpayers and create a more stable system, the most important reform is to never again be held hostage by institutions that pose a systemic risk and therefore have the power to tell us: "If you don't give us the money, we're going to blow up the whole system." Actually, what we have now is worse than a hostage system because in a classic hostage setup, after you pay the ransom you get the hostage back. We've paid more than a king's ransom, but have not taken the hostage -- our financial system -- back from the banks.

- Arianna Huffington: http://www.huffingtonpost.com/arianna-huffington/remember-that-whole-thing_b_252548.html

Bridging Banking and Philanthropy

A parallel network of smaller banks and its new social currency creates a bridge between the world of banking and the world of philanthropy. It builds upon precedents that already exist in both worlds and standardizes them into a system. Today many foundations extend what they call "program related investments." Conversely banks practice a form of involuntary philanthropy when they charge off bad debts.

Today hundreds of community based and private currencies already exist. California's IOUs (registered warrants) were one form of private currency. Reward programs, points, and airline miles are other forms of private currency. As long as enough people agree to use a currency then it has value as a medium of exchange.

The democratized, decentralized and digitized money and banking system in Capitalism 3.0 will catalyze a societal shift in priorities. To imagine such a system it is only necessary to think differently about the way money is created. This simple shift in thinking can inspire a new wave of wealth creation and introduce powerful economic incentives for whatever forms of societal improvement, economic benefit or ecological renewal we might imagine. Not all monetary systems are interest based, and not all monetary systems reward private interests quite as powerfully as our present monetary system.

> MONEY IS AN AGREEMENT WITHIN A COMMUNITY TO USE SOMETHING AS A MEDIUM OF EXCHANGE. THE AGREEMENT CAN BE CONSCIOUS OR UNCONSCIOUS, COERCED OR FREE. MOST OF US DON'T CONSCIOUSLY CHOOSE OUR MONEY. WE HAVE AN OPPORTUNITY TO CHANGE THAT. THE INTERNET IS A SPACE WHERE THAT IS POSSIBLE TO DO. I EXPECT A FLOURISHING OF MONEY SYSTEMS IN THE COMING YEARS. 95% OF THESE EXPERIMENTS WILL FAIL. BUT THE 5% THAT SUCCEED WILL CHANGE THE WORLD.
>
> - HOWARD RHEINGOLD, AUTHOR
> "THE INTERNET AND THE FUTURE OF MONEY"

Measuring the Unmeasurable

THE CREDIT COMMONS WILL ESTABLISH MARKETS AND MECHANISMS WILL ENABLE US TO MEASURE, MANAGE AND MONETIZE THE VALUE OF THINGS THAT OUR CURRENT BANK CENTRIC CURRENCY SYSTEM DOES NOT. ONE CAN THINK OF THE CREDIT COMMONS AS A CARBON CREDITS SYSTEM ON STEROIDS—EXTENDED TO THE WHOLE REALM OF HUMAN BEHAVIOR. IN THIS SYSTEM NEW AND SMALLER SOCIAL BANKS EMPOWERED TO CREATE BOTH DOLLARS AND THEIR OWN BRANDED CURRENCIES. LET'S CALL THESE CURRENCIES TOGETHER UNDER THE RUBRIC "SOCIAL DOLLARS."

SOCIAL DOLLARS ARE LIKE GOODWILL CIRCULATING IN MONETARY FORM PROVIDING A PERMANENT, STABLE AND SUSTAINABLE STIMULUS TO THE ECONOMY. WHAT WILL THIS ACCOMPLISH?

• Capitalism 3.0 will help us emerge from our current economic, social and environmental crises stronger than we ever were before.
• Capitalism 3.0 will awaken our slumbering economy without running up public debt.
• Capitalism 3.0 is an entirely new way of thinking about the most powerful tools ever created by humans: markets and money.
• Capitalism 3.0 introduces the idea of "blended value" into the equation that governs the way markets operate.
• Capitalism 3.0 will provide capital for clean technology, green business, social enterprise, venture philanthropy, social networking, social media and much more.

• Capitalism 3.0 will empower social entrepreneurs and non profits who are changing the world by providing access to mainstream capital markets for funding.

• Capitalism 3.0 will enable donors and investors to measure and monetize the value of "externalities" such as natural capital, social capital and equity.

• Capitalism 3.0 will compensate for the blind spots in financial markets.

• Capitalism 3.0 will restore stability and sustainability to the operations of Wall Street and balance their interests with the interests of Main Street.

• Capitalism 3.0 will enable us to redress the imbalances of our current financial system, create financial incentives to build a sustainable environment and improve the long term stability of financial markets.

• Capitalism 3.0 blends the notions of social impact with financial gain.

• Capitalism 3.0 marries the processes of creating private wealth with the processes of creating social value.

WHAT KIND OF SOCIETY DO WE WANT?

WHAT KIND OF SOCIETY DO WE WANT? WHAT DO PEOPLE NEED TO LEAD SATISFYING LIVES? ... OUR CURRENT SITUATION IS ONE NOT JUST OF DEEP ECONOMIC THREAT, WHICH IT SURELY IS, BUT ONE THAT ALSO CREATES A GREAT OPENING THROUGH " ...THE CRACK OF HISTORY..." FOR NATIONAL RENEWAL, AND A MORE MATURE SOCIETY ... EXPRESSED IN THE BROADEST POSSIBLE TERMS, "IS A HIGHER DEFINITION OF `LIFE, LIBERTY, AND THE PURSUIT OF HAPPINESS."

- WILLIAM R. NEIL IN HIS REVIEW OF WILLIAM GREIDER'S BOOK, COME HOME, AMERICA: THE RISE AND FALL (AND REDEEMING PROMISE) OF OUR COUNTRY

Monetizing the Value of Social and Natural Capital

Today markets are incapable of recognizing the value of "social capital" or "social equity." Economists often refer to social capital "externalities." The term externalities refers to something that is external to existing economic structure. What

exactly is social capital? Coming back to Einstein's quote, **"Not all things that count can be counted, and not all things that can be counted, count."** Einstein was talking about this question of value. What determines the value of something? In a market based economy, the market is the final arbiter of value. But markets draw little relationship between value and values. They don't recognize that what might be valuable to our environment or to society, can also have financial value.

This idea that has been around for some time in environmental and nonprofit circles, but it's just now beginning to sink into mainstream consciousness. In his 2007 commencement address at Harvard, Bill Gates talked about the tragedy taking place in parts of Africa, **"WE ASKED OURSELVES, CAN THE WORLD LET THESE CHILDREN DIE? THE ANSWER IS SIMPLE AND HARSH. THE MARKET DID NOT REWARD SAVING THE LIVES OF THESE CHILDREN AND GOVERNMENTS DID NOT SUBSIDIZE IT. SO THE CHILDREN DIED BECAUSE THEIR MOTHERS AND FATHERS HAD NO POWER IN THE MARKET AND NO VOICE IN THE SYSTEM. BUT YOU AND I HAVE BOTH. WE CAN MAKE MARKET FORCES WORK BETTER FOR THE POOR IF WE CAN DEVELOP A MORE CREATIVE FORM OF CREATIVE CAPITALISM."**

I HAVE A BACKGROUND MINDSET OF A MARKET SYSTEM. MARKETS HAVE WORKED AWFULLY WELL IN THIS COUNTRY, BUT MARKETS HAVE NOT WORKED FOR POOR PEOPLE AROUND THE WORLD WHO HAVE A DISEASE THAT CAN BE PREVENTED [IF THEY HAD JUST HAD SOME MEDICINE THAT IS AVAILABLE] FOR JUST PEANUTS REALLY.... THE MARKET JUST FAILS IN THAT CASE AND YOU HAVE TO INTERJECT YOURSELF INTO THAT, AND MAKE SURE THERE IS A SYSTEM THAT WILL DELIVER.

- WARREN BUFFETT

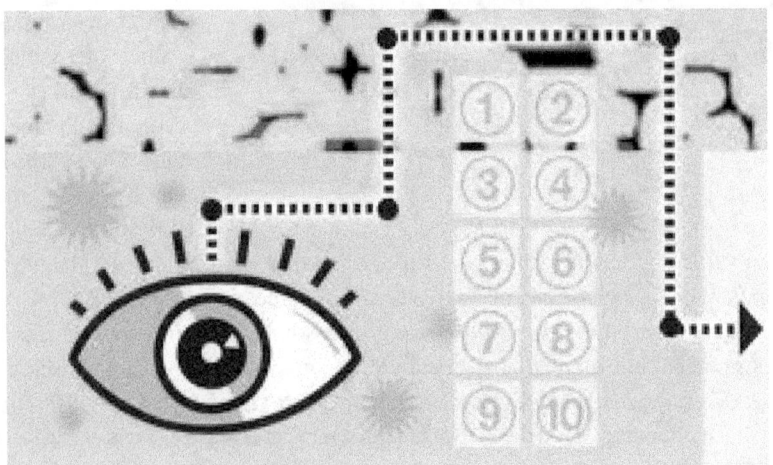

So markets have glaring blind spots: global health, global poverty, global environment to state a few. In each of these areas and many more, the problems have grown to a point of apparent intractability largely because the operating system for the global economy, has no way of valuing whatever a group or person is doing in the social interest. ... this so called social capital. It's the foundation of all social innovation.

Social capital exists throughout our society in various forms. Natural capital is a term that has been used extensively by environmentalists for years. Amory Lovins and Paul Hawken, in their book, appropriately titled Natural Capital, describes all kinds of activity that has value in protecting, promoting and preserving

the natural environment. Social and environmental equity capital today largely as metaphor because markets have no way to measure or monetize it. What cannot be measured or monetized gets thrown into this bucket we call philanthropy. A market mechanism like social dollars will enable the measurement and monetization of all forms of social capital including:

• **Community Capital:** is time spent advancing the goals or effectiveness of a community.

• **Family Capital:** is time devoted to helping a family grow and function as a living unit.

• **Natural Capital:** is anything that serves to protect, promote or preserve the natural environment.

• **Enterprise Capital:** is anything that enhances community standing of a corporate enterprise within society at large. Individuals can accumulate Enterprise Equity by helping to influence the modes or mindset of a company.

• **Educational Capital:** is anything that advances the state of learning or provides insight or elucidation.

• **Creative Capital:** is the creative energy expended by an author, artist, musician, filmmaker, video producer, photographer or editor in the process of creative expression.

• **Religious Capital:** is time dedicated to advancing the, meaningfulness, effectiveness or societal standing of a church congregation, synagogue, religious or spiritual community.

• **Social Network Capital:** is anything that that helps a network to grow or become more vital to members. Examples include time spent by members of a social network participating in network activities like blogging or music sharing.

• **Political Capital:** is time spent working on behalf of a political campaign or political cause.

• **Healing Capital:** is time or energy devoted to the healing arts in a community setting.

Now, let's focus on one particular form of social capital that has been generating interest lately in tech circles–Web based social capital–and see how it can be monetized through a a democratized Social Banking system that introduces a social currency like social dollars.

Monetizing the Value of Free

Wired Magazine editor, Chris Anderson, created a major controversy in the tech and business circles with the publication of his book, *"Free: The Future of a Radical Price."* With good reason! His thesis goes like a dagger right into the heart of the monetization strategy that has propelled the latest wave of Web 2.0 startups. If these startups have to give away for free what they provide, they have no business model, no revenues and no future as ongoing businesses. Investors will be out in the cold. BUT FREE NEED NOT BE FREE, IF THERE IS A TOOL FOR ITS MONETIZATION. SOCIAL DOLLARS IS JUST SUCH A TOOL. First, Chris Anderson's thesis in essence:

FREE! WHY $0.00 IS THE FUTURE OF BUSINESS

YOU KNOW THIS FREAKY LAND OF FREE AS THE WEB. A DECADE AND A HALF INTO THE GREAT ONLINE EXPERIMENT, THE LAST DEBATES OVER FREE VERSUS PAY ONLINE ARE ENDING. IN 2007 THE NEW YORK TIMES WENT FREE; THIS YEAR, SO WILL MUCH OF THE WALL STREET JOURNAL. (THE REMAINING FEE-BASED PARTS, NEW OWNER RUPERT MURDOCH ANNOUNCED, WILL BE "REALLY SPECIAL ... AND, SORRY TO TELL YOU, PROBABLY MORE EXPENSIVE." THIS CALLS TO MIND ONE VERSION OF STEWART BRAND'S ORIGINAL APHORISM FROM 1984: "INFORMATION WANTS TO BE FREE. INFORMATION ALSO WANTS TO BE EXPENSIVE ... THAT TENSION WILL NOT GO AWAY.") LOW-COST DIGITAL DISTRIBUTION WILL MAKE THE SUMMER BLOCKBUSTER FREE. THEATERS WILL MAKE THEIR MONEY FROM CONCESSIONS — AND BY SELLING THE PREMIUM MOVIEGOING EXPERIENCE AT A HIGH PRICE. ONCE A MARKETING GIMMICK, FREE HAS EMERGED AS A FULL-FLEDGED ECONOMY. OFFERING FREE MUSIC PROVED SUCCESSFUL FOR RADIOHEAD, TRENT REZNOR OF NINE INCH NAILS, AND A SWARM OF OTHER BANDS ON MYSPACE THAT GRASPED THE AUDIENCE-BUILDING MERITS OF ZERO. THE FASTEST-GROWING PARTS OF THE GAMING INDUSTRY ARE AD-SUPPORTED CASUAL GAMES ONLINE AND FREE-TO-TRY MASSIVELY MULTIPLAYER ONLINE GAMES. VIRTUALLY EVERYTHING GOOGLE DOES IS FREE TO CONSUMERS, FROM GMAIL TO PICASA TO GOOG-411. THE RISE OF "FREECONOMICS" IS BEING DRIVEN BY THE UNDERLYING TECHNOLOGIES THAT POWER THE WEB. JUST AS MOORE'S LAW DICTATES THAT A UNIT OF PROCESSING POWER HALVES IN PRICE EVERY 18 MONTHS, THE PRICE OF BANDWIDTH AND STORAGE IS DROPPING EVEN FASTER. WHICH IS TO SAY, THE TREND LINES THAT DETERMINE THE COST OF DOING BUSINESS ONLINE ALL POINT THE SAME WAY: TO ZERO.

- CHRIS ANDERSON, AUTHOR AND EDITOR OF WIRED MAGAZINE

If Anderson's thesis holds, it casts doubt on the future of online advertising and other revenue sources on the Web. Anderson laments that people seem to have misunderstood his thesis, because he had no intention of casting a pall over the future of the Internet. As Anderson points out, a deeper examination of free, suggests that giving something away can be a transition to a viable monetization strategy if it leads to the sale of something else. Google gives away search as a service to the Web, but it leads to revenues from advertisers who value click-throughs. *The Wall Street Journal* gives away the lead to its articles, in the hopes that people will pay to read more. The founders of social networks were amongst the first to recognize potential value of social and conversational capital. The more friends you have on Facebook, MySpace or LinkedIn, the more influential you seem to be. Influence can be translated into other things, but only if there is a vehicle for monetization.

THE NEW CURRENCY WON'T BE INTELLECTUAL CAPITAL. IT WILL BE SOCIAL CAPITAL-THE COLLECTIVE VALUE OF WHOM WE KNOW AND WHAT WE'LL DO FOR EACH OTHER. WHEN SOCIAL CONNECTIONS ARE STRONG AND NUMEROUS, THERE IS MORE TRUST, RECIPROCITY, INFORMATION FLOW, COLLECTIVE ACTION, HAPPINESS, AND, BY THE WAY, GREATER WEALTH.

JAMES KOUZES, CHAIRMAN EMERITUS OF TOM PETERS COMPANY, "LINK ME TO YOUR LEADER," BUSINESS 2.0 OCTOBER 10, 2000

Social dollars are a mechanism to translate the value of free into something of tangible value. Social Banks will create social dollars using a fractional reserve ratio, just like commercial banks create dollars when they make loans by leveraging the value of their deposits of dollars. Because retailers and others attach a value to social dollars in their product discounts, social dollars have value to users. If this sounds like hocus pocus, consider that it's the same hocus pocus that bankers use when they create money out of thin air by making accounting entries on their balance sheet in extending credit. Bankers don't have the money they lend out to borrowers, but borrowers still value what they have received in their loan. All it takes for the system to work is trust in the system, and an infrastructure to manage the transactions in social dollars. The development of such an infrastructure is inevitable, if the Web is to grow as a viable platform for business development. Why?

Today in the Web-based social networking and social media contexts there is untold value in social and conversational capital. The initiator of a Web-based conversation gets a return on their investment with increased exposure and stature. Marketers try to capitalize on this exposure, by enticing participants in the conversation to buy products. In that sense, conversation and the interest it generates is a currency. It's like the loans bankers make in dollars, and the return is like interest that bankers charge on their loans. Yet there is no mechanism to attach an economic value to this "social capital." Hence, it's mostly free.

With social dollars in circulation, suddenly there is a way to monetize the value of "free." In other words, the Web is evolving as we speak. There is too much capital and creativity now invested, for the darker side of Chris Anderson's hypothesis to hold. The need for mechanisms to monetize the value of what is progressing toward free will propel the development of a Web based social currency like social dollars and financial intermediaries like Social Banks to facilitate its flow.

THERE IS ALSO A BUSINESS CASE FOR SOCIAL CAPITAL - HARD EVIDENCE THAT SOCIAL CAPITAL BOOSTS BUSINESS PERFORMANCE. INDIVIDUALS WHO BUILD AND USE SOCIAL CAPITAL GET BETTER JOBS, BETTER PAY, FASTER PROMOTIONS, AND ARE MORE INFLUENTIAL AND EFFECTIVE, COMPARED WITH PEERS WHO ARE UNABLE OR UNWILLING TO TAP THE POWER OF SOCIAL CAPITAL. ORGANIZATIONS WITH RICH SOCIAL CAPITAL ENJOY ACCESS TO VENTURE CAPITAL AND FINANCING, IMPROVED ORGANIZATIONAL LEARNING, THE POWER OF WORD-OF-MOUTH MARKETING, THE ABILITY TO CREATE STRATEGIC ALLIANCES, AND THE RESOURCES TO DEFEND AGAINST HOSTILE TAKEOVERS. AND SOCIAL CAPITAL IS A BULWARK OF DEMOCRACY.

- WAYNE BAKER, AUTHOR
- ACHIEVING SUCCESS THROUGH SOCIAL CAPITAL

Awakening vs Stimulating the Economy

There's much talk these days about stimulating the economy, but little of the government money flowing towards Wall Street is flowing through to Main Street. There's something missing here. The very idea of stimulating the economy is flawed because it implies a temporary hit, like a fix, a sugar high, a drug or something artificial that works in the short term, but not in the long term. Like the historically low interest rates and lax lending standards that stimulated the housing and financial bubbles, we will inevitably face a reckoning with this "stimulus" strategy. It may provide a boost to stock prices. It may unthaw the banking system. It may help accelerate an upward trend out of the current crisis. There will be an overhang of public debt that one day we must deal with or live with the crushing economic burden of interest payments for generations to come.

Consider this unsettling reality: our banking system is infinitely leveraged. Leverage is simply another term for borrowing. Leveraged funds magnify the impact of relatively small swings in the marketplace. During good times, the leverage seems to be working to everyone's favor, but the rewards flow disproportionately to Wall Street banks. Seeking even higher levels of profit, banks are encouraged to take imprudent risks. For a while, they make really big money and nobody closely examines the risks they are welding into the system. Huge gains accrue 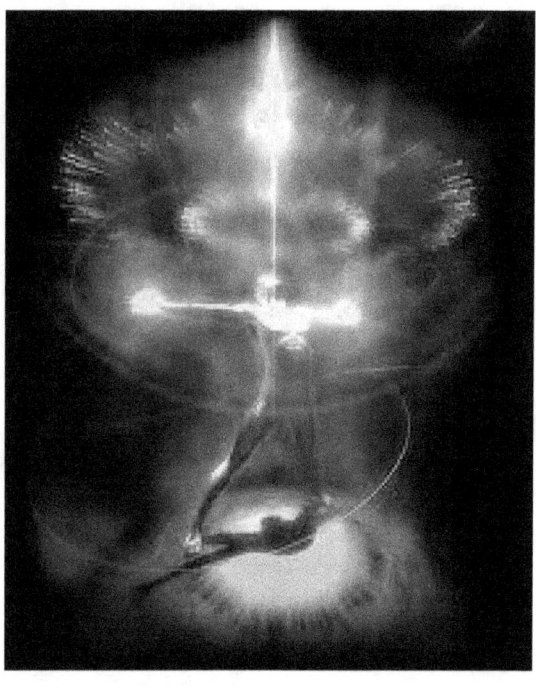 to investors and even bigger bonuses go to bankers and investment bankers. This pattern continues until, inevitably, the economy overreaches and heads into a downturn. Markets head south. Suddenly leverage starts working against everyone. Defaults soar and banks take losses, but their executives are still getting big bonuses despite reduce profitability or losses of the banks. Credit contracts and banking markets seize up. Then, because major banks are deemed "too big to fail", the government steps in to stabilize the banking system. The burden of covering the costs to stabilize the system now falls upon the taxpayer, and market based ideology is placed in abeyance until the next upturn. This is how *The 3C System* to *The Money Question* works in the favor of Wall Street bankers.

Now consider an alternative. *Capitalism 3.0* "awakens" the economy by leveling the playing field between Wall Street and Main Street. It will put the country on a path towards stable and sustainable growth. *Capitalism 3.0* thinks anew about the way that money is created and transfers some of the power now concentrated in commercial banks to a new network of public and social institutions. *Capitalism 3.0* democratizes the power to create money and decentralizes the power of our banking system so that no financial institution will ever again be "too big to fail." *Capitalism 3.0* goes deeper in our thinking to a point where we better understand the root causes of our current crisis, including inflationary pressures.

The Profound Shift in Markets and Values

The potential of this decentralized banking and monetary system is a reflection of changes that have been taking place in the marketplace. A profound shift is transforming consumer behavior and investor values. The full implications of this shift for markets are only beginning to be understood. This shift goes by different names: green business, social enterprise, social innovation, social networking, social marketing, social media, social capital, social finance, social investing and venture philanthropy. In their own way, each of these trends is powerful. Combined, this shift in thinking constitutes a sea change. What unites all these movements is the belief that there is 'something more' than what existing markets recognize, measure and value.

> NEVER LET A CRISIS GO TO WASTE! INSPIRED BY THE TRANSFORMATIVE IMPETUS OF THE ECONOMIC DOWNTURN, ... OUR CURRENT CRISIS IS ALSO A MORAL CRISIS, A FUNDAMENTAL CRISIS OF TRUST IN BUSINESS LEADERSHIP. ACCORDING TO THE CHICAGO BOOTH/KELLOGG SCHOOL FINANCIAL TRUST INDEX FROM APRIL 8, TRUST IN BUSINESS HAS REACHED UNPRECEDENTED LOWS, WITH ONLY 10% OF AMERICANS NOW SAYING THEY TRUST LARGE CORPORATIONS. THE "FUTURE OF CAPITALISM," IT SEEMS, IS AT STAKE. ALL THIS SERVES AS A CLARION CALL FOR BUSINESS AS UNUSUAL, AND NEW IDEAS AND VALUES ARE IN HIGH DEMAND.
>
> · BY TIM LEBERECHT, CNET NEWS
> MATTER/ANTI-MATTER, JULY 19, 2009

In our current system, there are trillions of dollars of value that markets are simply unable to measure, manage or monetize. These are glaring blind spots in our economic system. We need a vision that integrates these disparate trends into one powerful and cohesive movement: a movement that can be catalyzed by creating new markets and mechanisms that attach a value to the possibilities and potential that existing markets simply cannot see.

If we were to rebuild the idea of trust upon a new edifice – a "community of trust" that places a renewed faith in the future, it would be possible to integrate the above "social movements" into a cohesive structure. The structure will be linked by a "social" banking system operating in parallel to our primary banking system, Within this structure, it is entirely possible, that in a very short time, trillions dollars of previously unrecognized social value will be circulating through mainstream channels of commerce and community.

Shifting Our Trust To New Money and Markets

This idea of trust or the lack thereof has deep 'real world' and economic ramifications. From 2007 to 2009, approximately $10 trillion dollars of wealth eroded from the U.S. economic system. Where did all this money go? It vanished when bankers stopped trusting other bankers; lenders stopped trusting borrowers; people stopped trusting each other and institutionally, we stopped trusting in the future. The amount of wealth that exists at any moment is a function of highly subjective factors: consumer confidence, financial momentum, belief in the future, trust in each other, trust in the institutions of society. Indeed, the very solvency of our financial and banking system is founded on trust. Since our fiat based currency has no intrinsic worth, the value of our money and its derivative instruments is entirely a function of the trust we place in the system. Unfortunately, and perhaps even inevitably, trust in the system has eroded to a point where we must now think anew.

This is where social dollars and Social Banks come into play. They will provide a powerful stimulus to the overall economy because they can be very specifically targeted to those people, groups, and businesses that are vital to building a sustainable energy, economic, environmental and educational future. Suddenly schools, universities, non profits, community groups, social enterprises, churches, relief groups, NGOs, symphonies, artists, musicians and many more socially innovative groups will no longer be struggling to survive financially because they will have access to new sources of capital through this Social Banking system. Foundations will be able to magnify the impact of their giving in ways never before, by gaining access to financial leverage as Social Banks. This will enhance their collective power to meet the mounting and challenges they face.

Social Capital and Social Responsibility

WHILE ALL ORGANIZATIONS ATTEMPT TO CREATE VALUE OF ONE KIND OR ANOTHER, THE CENTRAL PREMISE OF THE BLENDED VALUE PROPOSITION IS THAT VALUE IS ITSELF A COMBINATION, A "BLEND" OF ECONOMIC, ENVIRONMENTAL AND SOCIAL FACTORS, AND THAT MAXIMIZING VALUE REQUIRES TAKING ALL THREE ELEMENTS INTO ACCOUNT. IN THE PAST, THERE HAS BEEN A REAL SEPARATION IN THE NOTIONS OF VALUE. CORPORATIONS HAVE SOUGHT TO MAXIMIZE ECONOMIC VALUE, WHILE PUBLIC INTEREST GROUPS HAVE SOUGHT TO MAXIMIZE SOCIAL OR ENVIRONMENTAL VALUE. HOWEVER, A GROWING GROUP OF PRACTITIONERS, INVESTORS AND PHILANTHROPISTS ARE ADVANCING STRATEGIES THAT INTENTIONALLY BLEND SOCIAL, ENVIRONMENTAL AND ECONOMIC VALUE. THESE ACTIVITIES HAVE RESULTED IN AN EXCITING WAVE OF NEW PRACTICES ACROSS THE FOR-PROFIT AND NONPROFIT SECTORS.
- BLENDED VALUE EXECUTIVE SUMMARY, OCTOBER 21, 2003 BY JED EMERSON AND SHEILA BONINI

Movements that were once disparate are now coalescing around common themes such as social capital, social responsibility and blended value. Providing quick view of this emerging landscape that will form a foundation for this community of trust, Jed Emerson and Sheila Bonini in their seminal whitepaper on "Blended Value" have identified five "silos" of activity that can form the nucleus of a "Community of Trust" for *Capitalism 3.0.*" They are:

1. CORPORATE SOCIAL RESPONSIBILITY (CSR) - THIS CATEGORY ENCOMPASSES CORPORATE CITIZENSHIP, CORPORATE ACCOUNTABILITY, BUSINESS ETHICS AND SUSTAINABILITY CAMPAIGNS. CSR DESCRIBES COMPANIES AND BUSINESS MANAGERS/LEADERS WHO CONSCIOUSLY INTEGRATE STRATEGIES THAT SEEK TO CREATE ENVIRONMENTAL AND SOCIAL VALUE WITHIN THEIR CORE BUSINESS MODELS, OPERATIONS AND SUPPLY CHAINS. CSR MAY ALSO REFER TO THE WAY A COMPANY MANAGES ITS INVESTMENTS AND PHILANTHROPY. IN DOING SO, CORPORATIONS USE MARKET RATE CAPITAL AND SEEK TO DELIVER MARKET-RATE, RISK ADJUSTED RETURNS.

2. SOCIAL ENTERPRISE (SE) - A USEFUL DEFINITION PROVIDED BY THE BRITISH GOVERNMENT DEFINES "SOCIAL ENTERPRISE" AS:

"BUSINESSES WITH PRIMARILY SOCIAL OBJECTIVES WHOSE SURPLUSES ARE PRINCIPALLY REINVESTED FOR THAT PURPOSE IN THE BUSINESS OR IN THE COMMUNITY, RATHER THAN BEING DRIVEN BY THE NEED TO MAXIMIZE PROFIT FOR SHAREHOLDERS AND OWNERS. SOCIAL ENTERPRISES TACKLE A WIDE RANGE OF SOCIAL AND ENVIRONMENTAL ISSUES AND OPERATE IN ALL PARTS OF THE ECONOMY.

3. SOCIAL INVESTING (SI) - SOCIAL INVESTING SEEKS FINANCIAL AND SOCIAL AND ENVIRONMENTAL RETURNS IN VARYING PROPORTIONS.

IT TYPICALLY INCLUDES THE FOLLOWING TWO CATEGORIES:

• SOCIALLY RESPONSIBLE INVESTING (SRI) - THROUGH INVESTMENT IN MUTUAL FUNDS AND ACTIVE PORTFOLIO MANAGEMENT, INVESTORS SEEK TO ACHIEVE MARKET-RATE RETURNS WHILE PROMOTING ENVIRONMENTAL AND/OR SOCIAL VALUES. FUND MANAGERS AND INVESTMENT ADVISORS CAN SCREEN PORTFOLIO INVESTMENTS AS WELL AS ENGAGE IN SHAREHOLDER ACTIVISM.

• COMMUNITY AND DOUBLE BOTTOM LINE INVESTING - IN THIS CASE, INVESTORS SEEK ECONOMIC, SOCIAL AND ENVIRONMENTAL VALUE BY PROVIDING MONEY TO COMMUNITY- DEVELOPMENT INSTITUTIONS OR PRIVATE EQUITY FUNDS. COMMUNITY INVESTING IS ACCOMPLISHED THROUGH GEOGRAPHICALLY FOCUSED STRATEGIES.

4. STRATEGIC PHILANTHROPY (SP) - STRATEGIC PHILANTHROPY (ALSO REFERRED TO AS "EFFECTIVE PHILANTHROPY") IS MARKED BY ITS COMMITMENT TO VIEWING PHILANTHROPY AS NOT SIMPLY AN APPROACH TO CHARITABLE GIVING, BUT RATHER TO INVESTING IN THE CREATION OF MEASURABLE SOCIAL IMPACT. WHILE STRATEGIC PHILANTHROPY REPRESENTS A SMALL PORTION OF OVERALL CHARITABLE GIVING, ITS FOCUS ON OUTCOMES AND ON CAPACITY-BUILDING PROVIDES PROMISE FOR THE FIELD AS A WHOLE.

5. SUSTAINABLE DEVELOPMENT (SD) - THIS TERM IS USED INTERCHANGEABLY WITH SUSTAINABLE CONSUMPTION AND PRODUCTION. THE GENERALLY ACCEPTED DEFINITION WAS PROPOSED BY THE UNITED NATIONS: "TO MEET THE NEEDS OF THE PRESENT WITHOUT COMPROMISING THE ABILITY OF FUTURE GENERATIONS TO MEET THEIR OWN NEEDS." THE WORLD BUSINESS COUNCIL ON SUSTAINABLE DEVELOPMENT (WBCSD) DEFINES SD IN TERMS OF THE COUNCIL'S COMMITMENT TO "SUSTAINABLE DEVELOPMENT VIA THE THREE PILLARS OF ECONOMIC GROWTH, ECOLOGICAL BALANCE AND SOCIAL PROGRESS."

REDEFINING CAPITAL

Umar Haique argues that we need o re-boot capitalism. And like Reinhard Marx, he focuses on a re-definition of "capital." His concept of "constructive capitalism," however, is more radical than the social market economy solution Marx proposes. Haique demands than the social market economy solution Marx proposes. Haique demands that 21st century economics fundamentally rethink "what capital isn't — and what capital really is." "The value equation of industrial-era capitalism was toxically imbalanced. Why is industrial era business so destructive — why does it slash and burn rainforests, endanger entire species, vaporize culture and community, marginalize the poor and disadvantaged, and erode our health and vitality? Because none of those have value in an industrial economy: none are capitalized. So the bean counters of the world are free to plunder and ruin them — because, economically they actually don't exist. 20th century capitalism, in other words, marginally valued pure financial capital too highly, while marginally valuing human, natural, social, and cultural capital at zero — or, at the limit, negatively." One example of the "capital deepening" Haique envisions are carbon assets: "Once they're capitalized, they become next-gen assets: assets that can be traded, hedged, remixed, tweaked, open-sourced, or shared. The difference is that they're assets with intrinsic, durable, human value — not the lemons Wall St was in the business of hawking. It is only by capitalizing the things we really value that the spark of value creation can be lit again." As another example of really valuable capital Haique refers to Rypple, an ad-hoc social network that provides simple, direct, anonymous, and ongoing customer and employee feedback: "Rypple's economic engine is powered by human and social capital — Rypple taps the connections people have with friends, colleagues, bosses, and mentors, to help them get smarter and more productive."

- by Tim Leberecht, CNET News - Matter/Anti-Matter, July 19, 2009

THE TRIPLE BOTTOM LINE

EDITED FROM WIKIPEDIA ARTICLE

THE TRIPLE BOTTOM LINE (OR "TBL", "3BL", OR "PEOPLE, PLANET, PROFIT") CAPTURES AN EXPANDED SPECTRUM OF VALUES AND CRITERIA FOR MEASURING ORGANIZATIONAL (AND SOCIETAL) SUCCESS: ECONOMIC, ECOLOGICAL AND SOCIAL. ... IN PRACTICAL TERMS, TRIPLE BOTTOM LINE ACCOUNTING MEANS EXPANDING THE TRADITIONAL REPORTING FRAMEWORK TO TAKE INTO ACCOUNT ECOLOGICAL AND SOCIAL PERFORMANCE IN ADDITION TO FINANCIAL PERFORMANCE. THE CONCEPT OF TBL DEMANDS THAT A COMPANY'S RESPONSIBILITY BE TO STAKEHOLDERS RATHER THAN SHAREHOLDERS. IN THIS CASE, 'STAKEHOLDERS' REFERS TO ANYONE WHO IS INFLUENCED, EITHER DIRECTLY OR INDIRECTLY, BY THE ACTIONS OF THE FIRM. ACCORDING TO THE STAKEHOLDER THEORY, THE BUSINESS ENTITY SHOULD BE USED AS A VEHICLE FOR COORDINATING STAKEHOLDER INTERESTS, INSTEAD OF MAXIMIZING SHAREHOLDER (OWNER) PROFIT. A TRIPLE BOTTOM LINE ENTERPRISE SEEKS TO BENEFIT MANY CONSTITUENCIES, NOT EXPLOIT OR ENDANGER ANY GROUP OF THEM. THE "UPSTREAMING" OF A PORTION OF PROFIT FROM THE MARKETING OF FINISHED GOODS BACK TO THE ORIGINAL PRODUCER OF RAW MATERIALS, I.E., A FARMER IN FAIR TRADE AGRICULTURAL PRACTICE, IS A NOT UNUSUAL FEATURE. IN CONCRETE TERMS, A TBL BUSINESS WILL NOT USE CHILD LABOUR AND MONITOR ALL CONTRACTED COMPANIES FOR CHILD LABOUR EXPLOITATION, WILL PAY FAIR SALARIES TO ITS WORKERS, WILL MAINTAIN A SAFE WORK ENVIRONMENT AND TOLERABLE WORKING HOURS, AND WILL NOT OTHERWISE EXPLOIT A COMMUNITY OR ITS LABOUR FORCE. A TBL BUSINESS ALSO TYPICALLY SEEKS TO "GIVE BACK" BY CONTRIBUTING TO THE STRENGTH AND GROWTH OF ITS COMMUNITY WITH SUCH THINGS AS HEALTH CARE AND EDUCATION. QUANTIFYING THIS BOTTOM LINE IS RELATIVELY NEW, PROBLEMATIC AND OFTEN SUBJECTIVE. THE GLOBAL REPORTING INITIATIVE (GRI) HAS DEVELOPED GUIDELINES TO ENABLE CORPORATIONS AND NGOS ALIKE TO COMPARABLY REPORT ON THE SOCIAL IMPACT OF A BUSINESS.

The Roots of Capitalism 3.0

THE NEW CORPORATION

WHAT ENABLES A CORPORATION TO SUCCEED IN THE LONGER TERM IS A WISH FOR IMMORTALITY, OR AT LEAST A LONG LIFE; A CONSISTENT SET OF VALUES BASED ON AN AWARENESS OF THE ORGANIZATION'S OWN IDENTITY; A WILLINGNESS TO CHANGE; AND A PASSIONATE CONCERN FOR DEVELOPING THE CAPABILITY AND SELF-CONFIDENCE OF ITS CORE INHABITANTS, WHOM THE COMPANY VALUES MORE THAN ITS PHYSICAL ASSETS. I SUGGEST THAT THOSE CONDITIONS ARE BEST MET WHEN ORGANIZATIONS LIVE UP TO THE LITERAL MEANING OF THE WORD COMPANY —'THE SHARING OF BREAD' — AND REGARD THEMSELVES AS COMMUNITIES, NOT PROPERTY.
- CHARLES HANDY, HARVARD BUSINESS REVIEW

The paradigms of modern business are changing. Consumers are demanding a voice in the marketplace and speaking with their wallets. A new generation of social entrepreneurs are baking in vanguard ideas into their business plans. Mutual responsibility, social and shared economies are changing the dynamics of marketing and selling. Transparency and community based ecosystems are becoming powerful forces in both the workplace and marketplace. Collaborative models are layered on top of competitive business models. New metrics are driving new kinds of businesses. Green is good and investors smell a new wave of wealth creation in clean tech. **These changes have not yet found their way into our money and banking system. This is the opening for Capitalism 3.0.**

THERE ARE NUMEROUS OTHER THINKERS THAT ENVISION A FASTER AND YET MORE SUSTAINABLE, SOCIAL BUSINESS AS THE FUTURE OF CAPITALISM, SOME RECURRING THEMES EMERGE THOUGH THE MORE YOU READ: ON THE ORGANIZATIONAL, DELIVERY SIDE, THESE THEMES ARE "SOCIAL," "REAL-TIME," AND "MICRO." AND ON THE CULTURAL, THE LEADERSHIP SIDE, THEY ARE "AUTHENTICITY," "GENEROSITY," AND "EMPATHY." IF YOU COMBINE THE TWO LAYERS, YOU GET AN INTERESTING MATRIX — LET'S CALL IT THE "MEANING-DRIVEN BUSINESS MATRIX."
- TIM LEBERECHT, FROG DESIGN AND CNET BLOG NETWORK

Capitalism 3.0 by Peter Barnes

Our current version of capitalism—the corporate, globalized version 2.0—is rapidly squandering our shared inheritances. Now, Peter Barnes offers a solution: protect the commons by giving it property rights and strong institutional managers. Barnes shows how capitalism—like a computer—is run by an

operating system. Our current operating system gives too much power to profit-maximizing corporations that devour our commons and distribute most of their profit to a sliver of the population. And government—which in theory should defend our commons—is all too often a tool of those very corporations. Barnes proposes a revised operating system—Capitalism 3.0—that protects the commons while preserving the many strengths of capitalism as we know it. His major innovation is the commons trust—a market-based entity with the power to limit use of scarce commons, charge rent, and pay dividends to everyone. Capitalism 3.0 offers a practical alternative to our current flawed economic system. It points the way to a future in which we can retain capitalism's virtues while mitigating its vices.

- Peter Barnes, Author: Capitalism 3.0 - A Guide To Reclaiming the Commons
http://capitalism3.com/

CON·SCIOUS   ADJ.

1. a. HAVING AN AWARENESS OF ONE'S ENVIRONMENT AND ONE'S OWN EXISTENCE, SENSATIONS, AND THOUGHTS. SEE SYNONYMS AT AWARE.
b. MENTALLY PERCEPTIVE OR ALERT; AWAKE:
2. CAPABLE OF THOUGHT, WILL, OR PERCEPTION: THE DEVELOPMENT OF CONSCIOUS LIFE ON THE PLANET.
3. SUBJECTIVELY KNOWN OR FELT: CONSCIOUS REMORSE.
4. INTENTIONALLY CONCEIVED OR DONE; DELIBERATE: A CONSCIOUS INSULT; MADE A CONSCIOUS EFFORT TO SPEAK MORE CLEARLY.
5. INWARDLY ATTENTIVE OR SENSIBLE; MINDFUL: WAS INCREASINGLY CONSCIOUS OF BEING WATCHED.

Capitalism 3.0 is a system where citizens consciously seize control of their own economic future rather than unconsciously submitting to market forces that they perceive to be beyond their control. This a form of capitalism is which participants are fully aware of the larger context in which their decisions are made. Today's form of capitalism is only partially conscious because citizens and business see themselves as slaves to a system. We make choices that don't reflect our interests because we think we have to. We do things that go against our interests because we see no other way. We degrade our natural environment because this is what the economic incentives of the market system motivate us to do. We give into a psychology that says the market is the master. *Capitalism 3.0* is an economic form of democracy. Bill Gates is promoting what he calls creative capitalism, which is a precursor of *Capitalism 3.0.* Here are some quotes from Bill Gates' speech at Davos, [2]

"WHY DO PEOPLE BENEFIT IN INVERSE PROPORTION TO THEIR NEED? WELL, MARKET INCENTIVES MAKE THAT HAPPEN. IN A SYSTEM OF CAPITALISM, AS PEOPLE'S WEALTH RISES, THE FINANCIAL INCENTIVE TO SERVE THEM RISES. AS THEIR WEALTH FALLS, THE FINANCIAL INCENTIVE TO SERVE THEM FALLS, UNTIL IT BECOMES ZERO. WE HAVE TO FIND A WAY TO MAKE THE ASPECTS OF CAPITALISM THAT SERVE WEALTHIER PEOPLE SERVE POORER PEOPLE AS WELL. THE GENIUS OF CAPITALISM LIES IN ITS ABILITY TO MAKE SELF-INTEREST SERVE THE WIDER INTEREST. THE POTENTIAL OF A

---

2 Remarks by Bill Gates, Chairman, Microsoft Corporation, World Economic Forum 2008, "A New Approach to Capitalism in the 21st Century," Davos, Switzerland, January 24, 2008

BIG FINANCIAL RETURN FOR INNOVATION UNLEASHES A BROAD SET OF TALENTED PEOPLE IN PURSUIT OF MANY DIFFERENT DISCOVERIES. THIS SYSTEM, DRIVEN BY SELF-INTEREST, IS RESPONSIBLE FOR THE INCREDIBLE INNOVATIONS THAT HAVE IMPROVED SO MANY LIVES.

GOODWILL CAPITALISM
BY VISH GOAD, PRESIDENT, WEBGEN CORPORATION

IN THE CURRENT SYSTEM, REVENUE GENERATING ACTIVITIES ARE REWARDED WITH MONEY AND OTHER ESSENTIAL BUT NON-REVENUE GENERATING ACTIVITIES ARE REWARDED WITH CERTIFICATES, MEDALS AND HONOR. BUT ONLY MONEY CAN GUARANTEE FOOD ON THE TABLE, TREATMENT FOR ILLNESSES AND A SOUND EDUCATION. GOODWILL CAPITALISM IS SET UP TO REWARD PEOPLE AND ACTIVITIES THAT ARE ESSENTIAL FOR BETTERMENT OF THE SOCIAL FABRIC EVEN IF THEY DO NOT DIRECTLY CONTRIBUTE TO REVENUES. GOODWILL CAPITALISM IS PROPOSED AS A SECONDARY ECONOMIC SYSTEM TO THE CURRENT MONEY BASED ECONOMY, IN WHICH THE GOODWILL GENERATED BETWEEN ANY TWO ENTITIES (PEOPLE, BUSINESSES, GOVERNMENT ETC.) IS QUANTIFIED, TRACKED AND USED AS A MEDIUM OF EXCHANGE IN COMMERCIAL TRANSACTIONS. THE UNIT OF MEASUREMENT OF GOODWILL IS CALLED GOODWILL CREDIT OR GEECEE, AS WE WILL REFER TO IT FROM HERE ON. GOODWILL CAPITALISM IS CONCEIVED WITH THE EXPRESS PURPOSE OF GUARANTEEING BASIC QUALITY OF LIFE AND LIFESTYLES TO EVERY PERSON REGARDLESS OF THEIR PERCEIVED STATUS AS A "PRODUCTIVE" MEMBER OF THE SOCIETY. THE WORD "PRODUCTIVE" IS USED HERE IN THE TRADITIONAL CONTEXT OF MONEY BASED ECONOMY THAT IMPLIES PARTICIPATING IN AND CONTRIBUTING TO REVENUE GENERATING TASKS AND ACTIVITIES. GOODWILL CAPITALISM WILL ACCOMPLISH THIS OBJECTIVE BY MONETIZING SOCIAL RELATIONSHIPS, HUMAN AND SOCIAL CAPITAL USING GOODWILL CAPITAL A RESOURCE THAT NEVER RUNS OUT.

BUT TO HARNESS THIS POWER SO IT BENEFITS EVERYONE, WE NEED TO REFINE THE SYSTEM. AS I SEE IT, THERE ARE TWO GREAT FORCES OF HUMAN NATURE: SELF-INTEREST, AND CARING FOR OTHERS. CAPITALISM HARNESSES SELF-INTEREST IN A HELPFUL AND SUSTAINABLE WAY, BUT ONLY ON BEHALF OF THOSE WHO CAN PAY. GOVERNMENT AID AND PHILANTHROPY CHANNEL OUR CARING FOR THOSE WHO CAN'T PAY. BUT TO PROVIDE RAPID IMPROVEMENT FOR THE POOR WE NEED A SYSTEM THAT DRAWS IN INNOVATORS AND BUSINESSES IN A FAR BETTER WAY THAN WE DO TODAY.

SUCH A SYSTEM WILL HAVE A TWIN MISSION: MAKING PROFITS AND ALSO IMPROVING LIVES OF THOSE WHO DON'T FULLY BENEFIT FROM TODAY'S MARKET FORCES. FOR SUSTAINABILITY WE NEED TO USE PROFIT INCENTIVES WHEREVER WE CAN. AT THE SAME TIME, PROFITS ARE NOT ALWAYS POSSIBLE WHEN BUSINESS TRIES TO SERVE THE VERY POOR. IN SUCH CASES THERE NEEDS TO BE ANOTHER INCENTIVE, AND THAT INCENTIVE IS RECOGNITION. RECOGNITION ENHANCES A COMPANY'S REPUTATION AND APPEALS TO CUSTOMERS; ABOVE ALL, IT ATTRACTS GOOD PEOPLE TO AN

ORGANIZATION. AS SUCH, RECOGNITION TRIGGERS A MARKET-BASED REWARD FOR GOOD BEHAVIOR. IN MARKETS WHERE PROFITS ARE NOT POSSIBLE, RECOGNITION IS A PROXY; WHERE PROFITS ARE POSSIBLE, RECOGNITION IS AN ADDED INCENTIVE. ...

THE CHALLENGE HERE IS TO DESIGN A SYSTEM WHERE MARKET INCENTIVES, INCLUDING PROFITS AND RECOGNITION, DRIVE THOSE PRINCIPLES TO DO MORE FOR THE POOR. I LIKE TO CALL THIS IDEA CREATIVE CAPITALISM, AN APPROACH WHERE GOVERNMENTS, BUSINESSES, AND NONPROFITS WORK TOGETHER TO STRETCH THE REACH OF MARKET FORCES SO THAT MORE PEOPLE CAN MAKE A PROFIT, OR GAIN RECOGNITION, DOING WORK THAT EASES THE WORLD'S INEQUITIES.

SOME PEOPLE MIGHT OBJECT TO THIS KIND OF MARKET-BASED SOCIAL CHANGE, ARGUING THAT IF WE COMBINE SENTIMENT WITH SELF-INTEREST, WE WILL NOT EXPAND THE REACH OF THE MARKET, BUT REDUCE IT. YET ADAM SMITH, THE VERY FATHER OF CAPITALISM AND THE AUTHOR OF "WEALTH OF NATIONS," WHO BELIEVED STRONGLY IN THE VALUE OF SELF-INTEREST FOR SOCIETY, OPENED HIS FIRST BOOK WITH THE FOLLOWING LINES: "HOW SELFISH SOEVER MAN MAY BE SUPPOSED, THERE ARE EVIDENTLY SOME PRINCIPLES IN HIS NATURE, WHICH INTEREST HIM IN THE FORTUNES OF OTHERS, AND RENDER THEIR HAPPINESS NECESSARY TO HIM, THOUGH HE DERIVES NOTHING FROM IT, EXCEPT THE PLEASURE OF SEEING IT."

CREATIVE CAPITALISM TAKES THIS INTEREST IN THE FORTUNES OF OTHERS AND TIES IT TO OUR INTEREST IN OUR OWN FORTUNES IN WAYS THAT HELP ADVANCE BOTH. THIS HYBRID ENGINE OF SELF-INTEREST AND CONCERN FOR OTHERS CAN SERVE A MUCH WIDER CIRCLE OF PEOPLE THAN CAN BE REACHED BY SELF-INTEREST OR CARING ALONE. ...

ANOTHER APPROACH TO CREATIVE CAPITALISM INCLUDES A DIRECT ROLE FOR GOVERNMENTS. OF COURSE, GOVERNMENTS ALREADY DO A GREAT DEAL TO HELP THE POOR IN WAYS THAT GO FAR BEYOND JUST NURTURING MARKETS: THEY FUND AID RESEARCH, HEALTHCARE; THEY'VE DONE GREAT THINGS. BUT I

BELIEVE THE HIGHEST-LEVERAGE WORK THAT GOVERNMENTS CAN DO IS TO SET POLICY TO CREATE MARKET INCENTIVES FOR BUSINESS ACTIVITY THAT IMPROVES THE LIVES OF THE POOR. ...

FINALLY, ONE OF THE MOST INVENTIVE FORMS OF CREATIVE CAPITALISM INVOLVES SOMEONE WE ALL KNOW VERY WELL. A FEW YEARS AGO, I WAS SITTING IN A BAR HERE IN DAVOS WITH BONO. LATE AT NIGHT, AFTER A FEW DRINKS, HE WAS ON FIRE, TALKING ABOUT HOW WE CAN GET A PERCENTAGE OF EACH PURCHASE FROM CIVIC-MINDED COMPANIES TO HELP CHANGE THE WORLD. HE KEPT CALLING PEOPLE, WAKING THEM UP, AND HANDING ME THE PHONE TO SHOW ME THE INTEREST. WELL, IT'S TAKEN TIME TO GET THIS GOING, BUT HE WAS RIGHT. IF YOU GIVE PEOPLE A CHANCE TO ASSOCIATE THEMSELVES WITH A CAUSE THEY CARE ABOUT, WHILE BUYING A GREAT PRODUCT, THEY WILL. ...

THERE IS A GROWING UNDERSTANDING AROUND THE WORLD THAT WHEN CHANGE IS DRIVEN BY PROPER INCENTIVES, YOU HAVE A SUSTAINABLE PLAN FOR CHANGE, BECAUSE PROFITS AND RECOGNITION ARE RENEWABLE RESOURCES. ... THIS IS A WORLD-WIDE MOVEMENT, AND WE ALL HAVE THE ABILITY AND THE RESPONSIBILITY TO ACCELERATE IT. ... FINALLY, I HOPE THAT THE GREAT THINKERS HERE WILL DEDICATE SOME TIME TO FINDING WAYS FOR BUSINESSES, GOVERNMENTS, NGOS, AND THE MEDIA TO CREATE MEASURES OF WHAT COMPANIES ARE DOING TO USE THEIR POWER AND INTELLIGENCE TO SERVE A WIDER CIRCLE OF PEOPLE. THIS KIND OF INFORMATION IS AN IMPORTANT ELEMENT OF CREATIVE CAPITALISM. IT CAN TURN GOOD WORKS INTO RECOGNITION, AND ENSURE THAT RECOGNITION BRIDGES MARKET-BASED REWARDS TO BUSINESSES THAT DO THE MOST WORK TO SERVE THE MOST PEOPLE.

WE ARE LIVING IN A PHENOMENAL AGE. IF WE CAN SPEND THE EARLY DECADES OF THE 21ST CENTURY FINDING APPROACHES THAT MEET THE NEEDS OF THE POOR IN WAYS THAT GENERATE PROFITS AND RECOGNITION FOR BUSINESS, WE WILL HAVE FOUND A SUSTAINABLE WAY TO REDUCE POVERTY IN THE WORLD. THE TASK IS OPEN-ENDED. IT WILL NEVER BE FINISHED. BUT A PASSIONATE EFFORT TO ANSWER THIS CHALLENGE WILL HELP CHANGE THE WORLD.

Because of Bill Gates' stature, his words are a great cause for optimism that our economic system can be updated in time to avert a reckoning. Even Bill Gates tends to circumscribe his thinking in the boundaries of convention. With the resources The Bill and Melinda Gates Foundation is bringing to bear in addressing social issues, they are still just nibbling around the edges of problems that are staggering in magnitude. In due time Bill Gates and his foundation will soon learn that the billions of dollars they have dedicated to worthy and carefully considered social initiatives are inadequate. Why? Because they are not addressing the root cause of our current problems at it's core: the nature of money itself and how it is created. *Capitalism 3.0* is broader and deeper than creative capitalism. *Capitalism 3.0* takes a hard look at aspects of the market based economy that have been off limits to the mainstream of economic thought. Ultimately we must realize that it is conventional thinking that has brought us to this point.

Bill Gates' creative capitalism is a way for the rich to help the poor. It is all well and good, but what about all the people on Main Street who are hurting? What about all the consumers, businesses and municipal governments can't make ends meet and have no choice other than to live from month to month without considering the longer term consequences of their decisions. What about all of those who are running of the treadmill, going deeper and deeper into debt? What about all the small business owners who are struggling to survive? What about the students who can't find the money they need to continue their education?

Creative capitalism is a good start in the right direction, but it is not comprehensive. *Capitalism 3.0* is more far reaching than creative capitalism because it considers a broader context. *Capitalism 3.0* considers revisions to our system that are more fundamental, because it democratizes our entire financial system. Bill Gates and his creative capitalism is a light dose of reform. We need something stronger. *Capitalism 3.0* is a fundamental solution to a fundamental problem. Here is how it will work to the benefit of us all.

> TO TRANSFORM SOMETHING IS TO CHANGE IN A FUNDAMENTAL WAY ITS NATURE OR FUNCTION. ONCE YOU HAVE CHANGED THE NATURE AND FUNCTION OF YOUR INTERACTION WITH MONEY, ... YOUR RELATIONSHIP WITH MONEY WILL BE TRANSFORMED—YOU WILL REACH NEW LEVEL OF COMFORT, COMPETENCE AND CONSCIOUSNESS AROUND MONEY. AND THAT'S ONLY THE BEGINNING OF WHAT IS POSSIBLE—ONCE YOU START FOLLOWING THIS NEW ROAD MAP FOR MONEY.
>
> - JOE DOMINGUEZ AND VICKI ROBIN, AUTHORS, YOUR MONEY OR YOUR LIFE: TRANSFORMING YOUR RELATIONSHIP WITH MONEY AND ACHIEVING FINANCIAL INDEPENDENCE.

A Better Way Out of Debt

What if we could turn our social capital — like helping a neighbor — into real money?

Can social capital redeem our financial souls? At a time when financial markets have clearly let us down, we can't afford to breathe new life into a carcass. Social capital offers the solution we have been looking for. What is social capital? It refers to the worth of our social networks, individual skills, and even things like the time we invest in volunteering. For example, the time I put into helping a neighbor paint a fence (free of charge) is a form of social capital. Its value equates to the time I spent and the "worth" of an enhanced relationship. In traditional economics, the nonfinancial contributions we make are basically worthless. Financial transactions and our monetary net worth are all that really matter. Sadly, we have sunk to measuring our individual and national value through debt, surpluses, and productivity gains. But what if we looked beyond investments and financial capital and began taking social capital seriously? It's really not that hard to put a quantitative value on any number of seemingly intangible assets. One hour of my volunteer time could easily be quantified as $10. And an open reputation system, similar to Amazon bookseller ratings, could help to measure and quantify our standing as social citizens. Here's a novel idea: What if credit-card companies and financial institutions invented a system to measure social capital and include it in your monthly statements? This would provide a more comprehensive way to measure and understand our overall worth. By combining financial and social capital we could see a more accurate picture of our true value. With this holistic model in place, reading your financial statements wouldn't be such a painful monthly ritual. In addition, it would also offer an important incentive to give and borrow more, particularly if you and I were rewarded for such activities. Marrying financial transactions with social transactions, in the form of a "social credit card," would undoubtedly encourage wiser spending and saving habits. Frequent Giving Points could be exchanged for real goods and services — similar to frequent flier miles. A whole new form of exchange would emerge, redeemable by and tradable between individuals — putting us more squarely in the driver's seat of how we spend our time and money. For those in debt, social capital points could be used to pay down all or a portion of what they owe. I'd line up to open a social credit card or social savings account. Wouldn't you? The benefits would not only be spiritual and personal but also practical and collective. Individually, we'd pour new energy into being good neighbors. Collectively, we'd transform social capital into a lasting economic stimulus. So let's get going on leveraging our social capital in new and exciting ways. The White House has called for social innovation and a new age of volunteerism. This radical idea offers a way to boldly promote both. We are so much more than our credit cards and bank accounts would have us believe. And the last time I considered my worth as a human being, the stock market did not readily come to mind. Greed is no longer the answer. If today's economic troubles are rooted in a credit crisis, let's start digging ourselves out by giving more credit — to ourselves.

- Paul Lamb, Principal of Man on a Mission Consulting

Decentralizing the Money System

The debate today on how best to stimulate the economy has been circumscribed by the notion that the control of the money supply and banking system must be centralized. A truly sustainable economic recovery would incorporate both centralized and decentralized approaches to creating liquidity in the financial system. If we were to think in bold new terms it is possible to imagine a multitiered money and banking system in which not only central governments and banks, but also government agencies, state governments, municipalities, businesses, universities, foundations, churches, community groups and non profits can create money. In this parallel money system, the money power becomes a continuum, extending from large private banks to smaller and more publicly oriented institutions.

What will it take for such a multitiered money and banking system to work? There are four essential elements of any viable monetary system:
- Trust in the system.
- A fungible commodity to serve as the medium of exchange: i.e. social dollars.
- A mechanism for exchange of social dollars.
- A means to maintain the value of social dollars.

This Credit Commons a democratized, decentralized and digitized banking system that acts as a flywheel to the centralized, concentrated and commercialized money and banking system. It extends the power to create money to other private, public and social entities like foundations, universities, non profits, small businesses, social service groups, social enterprises – entities that are acting in the larger interests of society, sustainability, economic stability and social justice. These groups normally would find the process of creating back end banking infrastructure daunting, but with cloud computing they can simply adopt and apply existing plug and play architecture developed by the social reserve banking system.

A New Psychology of Money

Let's now take a few step back from the mechanics of the system and consider what it accomplishes in a social and cultural context. Throughout history there have been two great forces sparring with each other. The first is the competitive spirit. It's the competitive fire that dominates the psychology of sports, warfare, business, markets and so much else in our lives. There is something deep within our psyche that propels us to somehow prevail, to demonstrate that we are better, smarter, stronger, more skilled or more powerful than the opposition or enemy. Then, there is the collaborative or and egalitarian instinct. This urge helps us blend into community, collaborate, share our skills and resources to elevate us as a civilized society than can mesh goals and visions.

In traditional commercial banking, the competitive spirit has dominated largely because it is burned into the DNA of both individual bankers and the system.

The internal dynamics of this complementary banking and monetary system will create an entirely different psychology of money; one that will effect the culture as a whole and everyone within it. On a societal level, it will be a psychology of community, caring and compassion as goodwill circulates through the economy in monetary form as social dollars. On a structural level, it will promote the power of doing good and leverage scarce resources presently available to the social sector. On an individual level, it will help create a psychology of cooperation and collaboration rather than the current psychology of indebtedness; and on a financial level, it will promote economic stability in place of the anxiety and risk that characterize a system based on the issuance of debt.

No longer will banks and governments have a monopoly over the creation of money. With the arrival of the Internet, and private payment systems like Paypal and Google Checkout, it is now possible to route all transactions of social dollars in digital form. This structure will help to stabilize the central banking system because the money created will help reduce default rates. For this reason it is in the self interest of governments and commercial banks to support it. Transactions of the social currency can even be accounted for through existing banking and credit card channels, providing a supplemental income stream for them.

The buying power of the social currency will be maintained by the marketplace. Social dollars will be offered as discounts by corporate retailers participating in the system. Thus, social dollars can be used and redeemed during of normal shopping at supermarkets and retailers, both online and offline. For example, when a consumer goes through the checkout line at the supermarket, and uses a social credit card issued by a participating bank, automatically they earn or redeem social dollars as discounts. Social dollars can also be exchanged for points, airline miles or rewards in private corporate currency systems. The system will be entirely voluntary so anyone will have the right to opt out by rejecting the social currency. At any time social dollars will be exchangeable for official government currencies on a secondary trading exchange.

The ability to create social dollars can be tailored to meet pressing social, economic and environmental needs. In other words, part of the criteria for becoming certified as a Social Bank will be the need to articulate some overriding social, economic or environmental objective in issuing the social dollars. It democratizes the power to create money in the same way that the Internet has democratized the power to create news.

THE BANK OF YOU AND ME

As in times past, like the populist era of the late nineteenth century, the business people, farmers, and others engaged in productive enterprise are clamoring to gain access to credit -- credit which they fail to recognize is already theirs. Under the present arrangements, we give our credit to the banks then beg them to lend some of it back to us -- at interest. The real solution lies in creating new structures for allocating credit based on the legitimate needs of businesses, workers, and state and local governments. Is there any practical possibility of organizing on a sufficiently large scale to achieve this? I maintain that there is; that in fact, it is far more practical, likely, and empowering than any political reform of money and banking currently on offer. America's greatness has always stemmed from the creativity, industriousness, and goodwill of its people. Ours is a cooperative, compassionate, "can do" society.

I believe that we can create exchange alternatives based on voluntary, free-market and community-based initiatives that enable people to transcend the money monopoly and the "war machine." Socially responsible businesses and social entrepreneurs have a crucial role to play in organizing these parallel systems that can shift enough power to achieve greater measures of independence and self-determination and bring enormous benefits across the board -- social, political, economic, environmental, and cultural. The primary objective of an exchange alternative should be to utilize the credit of local producers to mediate the exchange of goods and services locally. The bottom line is that non-bank exchange system credits and community currencies must be issued in ways that monetize the value inherent in goods and services being exchanged. This means they must be "spent" into circulation, not "sold" into circulation. With regard to the various alternative exchange systems and community currencies that have been tried so far, almost all have been designed to solve secondary problems, or have been lacking in scalability. ...

- Thomas Greco,
Author: The End of Money and the Future of Civilization
http://www.alternet.org/workplace/141582/the_end_of_money
%3a_take_power_back_from_the_money_and_banking_monopol
y?page=entire

Let's Imagine What This Could Turn Into

Your School's Social Bank - Your local school's Social Bank issues social dollars to parents of students who get involved in their child's education. Those parents use the social dollars to obtain discounts with merchants or to pay for a portion of their child care and preschool expenses. The child care center uses the social dollars to supplement the income of their staff. The staff members use social dollars to receive discounts at local merchants, reduce their interest charges on their credit card, auto finance loan or mortgage. If they rent an apartment at a participating low income project, they can use social dollars to help pay the rent.

The Social Dollar Empowerment Exchange: XYZ Social Bank issues social  dollars to schools. Those schools establish criteria and a procedure for recognizing exceptional teachers or parents who demonstrate their commitment to their child's educational development. Schools award social dollars as an income supplement to reward exceptional teachers and parents. Staff members use social dollars to receive discounts at local merchants, reduce their interest charges on their credit card, auto finance loan or mortgage. If they rent an apartment at a participating low income project, they can use social dollars to help pay the rent. They can also use social dollars as partial payment for goods or services they buy online at a "Social Dollar Empowerment Exchange."

Affordable Housing's Social Bank: The Affordable Housing Social Bank issues social dollars as an economic incentive to a real estate developer to proceed with an affordable housing project. That developer uses the social dollars to compensate neighbors of the proposed project for any perceived decrease in property values, increase in traffic, noise or other unwanted consequences of the proposed project. Those neighbors can use the social dollars to reduce their interest rates on mortgages, credit card or consumer loans. They can also use the social dollars to obtain discounts at supermarkets, department stores and local merchants.

Rental Payment Social Bank: The Renters Social Bank issues social dollars to citizens who can verify that they quality for low income status. Those qualifying citizens use social dollars to help pay rent. The landlord uses the social dollars to reduce interest payments on loans from participating banks. The banks use the social dollars to create incentives to customers to open new checking or credit card accounts / increase deposits in existing accounts.

Example Number 5 - Financial Incentives to Employers Who Hire Low Income Residents: The Low Income Social Bank issues social dollars to employers as a financial incentive to hire qualifying low income residents. Those employers use their social dollars to:
- Offer discounts in social dollars to their customers.
- Obtain below market interest rates on small business loans from banks.
- Provide an income supplement to other employees working at their company.
- Create economic incentives for employees who bicycle, carpool or take public transportation to work.
- Create economic incentives for employees can demonstrate that they have reduced their carbon footprint or undertaken water conservation measures.

Low Income Social Bank: The Low Income Social Bank issues social dollars as income supplements to residents who can demonstrate their low income status. Those residents use their social dollars to help pay rent at participating housing projects. Owners of those housing projects use social dollars to obtain reduced interest expense at participating banks. The banks use the social dollars to create economic incentives for people to open checking, saving or credit card accounts at the bank.

"Curb Your Carbon" Social Bank: The Curb Your Carbon Social Bank issues social dollars to the "Curb your Carbon" group. "Curb your Carbon" allocates a portion of their social dollars allotment to schools and area businesses. The schools and businesses issue social dollars to employees, students and staff who undertake various efforts to reduce their carbon footprint such as bicycling to work/school, carpooling and taking public transportation. Curb your Carbon also issues a "Carbon Footprint Smartcard" containing an allocation of social dollars to residents when they reduce their carbon consumption.

Environmental Education Social Bank: The Ecology Social Bank issues social dollars to environmental non profits. Those groups issue social dollars as an income supplement to staff, board members and volunteers. The staff member use social dollars to receive discounts at local merchants, reduce their interest charges on their credit card, auto finance loan or mortgage. If they rent an apartment at a participating low income project they can use social dollars to help pay the rent.

B2B Credit Union - Many businesses all realize that they will need additional funds to avoid bankruptcy and cannot obtain credit from their local banks. They also realize that they are part of the same supply chain and routinely sell goods and services to each other. They agree to use social dollars to establish a mutual credit cooperative whereby they can provide credit to each others without the intervention of banks. They accomplish this and avoid the burden of interest payments on the credits they extend to each other.

Student Loan Social Bank: The Student Loan Social Bank helps university students who are unable to obtain student loans and are forced to drop out of school. The university becomes a Social Bank and obtains authority to issue social dollars to students who are working in various part time staff, coaching, tutoring and mentoring roles in the community. These social dollars are sufficient to enable the students to continue their education while helping out the community.

The Social Enterprise Fund: The partners at XYZ Venture Capital Fund realize they are only investing in startups that provide little benefit to society or the environment. The pressure to obtain above market returns forces them to discount any social benefits of their potential investments. They decide to form a Social Bank. The VC Social Bank issue social dollars to existing portfolio companies who have ideas for alternative energy sources in new energy markets that have not yet reached market maturity but that have social or environmental benefit. The social dollars are used by the startups to provide incentives for customers to buy their sources of alternative energy even though it presently costs a bit more than conventional energy.

What Else Can You Think Of?

- The Sierra Club issues social dollars to people to use energy efficient light bulbs.
- Communities issue social dollars to parents who volunteer to coach or referee sports teams.
- Companies issue social dollars to employees who carpool or ride a bicycle to work.
- Municipalities issue social dollars to people who reduce fire hazards around their home.
- Relief groups issue social dollars to victims of national disasters.
- Companies issue social dollars at point of purchase to shoppers who buy green products.
- Governments issue social dollars to people who buy hybrid cars.
- Symphonies accept social dollars as discounts for people who attend concerts.
- Elder care facilities issue social dollars to people who volunteer to help residents.
- Municipalities issue social dollars to home owners who use alternative energy sources.
- Non-profits issue social dollars to donors or people who agree to serve on their board.
- Community health clinics accept social dollars as partial payment for treatment.
- Stores accept social dollars from homeless people to buy basic necessities.
- Supermarkets issue social dollars to shoppers who choose to use paper or cloth bags.
- Utilities issue social dollars to people who conserve energy or buy their energy from renewable energy companies.
- Governments issues social dollars as an income supplement to people who are not on welfare, but who are in danger of going on welfare.
- During the periods of currency panic, social dollars can serve as an alternative medium of exchange.
- In response to a natural disaster social dollars can provide supplemental and immediate relief to victims without incurring additional public debt. In such a situation national businesses will be encouraged to honor social dollars in partial exchange for goods.

THE LIST CAN GO ON AND ON.

Moderating The Risks of Inflation

To avoid inflation, the economy must grow commensurate with the money supply. But where will the growth in the U. S. economy come from? One of the most significant potential areas of growth is the social economy. Economists estimate that over $2 trillion dollars of economic activity that current takes place in the social economy is not currently measured or monetized by markets.

The challenge then is to find a vehicle to recognize this unmeasured activity. This is the essence of the social currency in *Capitalism 3.0*. It is a mechanism to measure and monetize trillions of dollars of unrecognized economic activity. Thus the introduction of social dollars expands the economy without creating inflation. The growth in the money supply with social dollars is matched by the growth in goods and services from the social economy. This is a win-win scenario, awakening the economy without inflationary pressure.

This network of public and Social Banks could act as a counterweight to the instabilities, inadequacies, imbalances and inequities of the current banking system. The Social Banking system will introduce the power of leverage and provide access to capital for areas of the economy that are currently starved of the resources they need to create a healthy, sustainable, educated, environmentally sound and economically just society. If this can be accomplished, it will be possible to both stimulate the mainstream economy and catalyze a new wave of wealth creation out of value that the market currently doesn't recognize.

The manner in which money is created by banks today has deep psychological effects on the way we interact with each other. It creates a psychology of competition rather than a psychology of cooperation. It also isn't very effective in providing the right stimuli at the right time. The current banking system expands the supply of credit when the economy when it needs it least: when consumer and business confidence is highest. Conversely, the banking system contracts when people and business most need credit. The current system provides capital to the people who need it least: the people who already have capital or access to capital and the system doesn't provide credit to economically strapped individuals and businesses when they need it most. By democratizing the power to create money through Social Banks and introducing social dollars to monetize social equity, the supply of goods and services in the overall economy is increased thus moderating the inflationary effects of increased government borrowing.

The Systemic Benefits of the Credit Commons

First, it is possible to finely tune the cost of capital to Social Banks depending on how much social, environmental or economy benefit they are creating with their social dollars. This control over the cost of capital can target the use of social dollars much more specifically than the current 3C money system.

Second, it will provide capital to the people, businesses and groups who need it most, when they need it most. It will stimulate the economy during times when the economy most needs to be stimulated. The current system does just the opposite. The current system stimulates the economy when it needs it least: when consumer and business confidence is highest. The current system provides capital to the people who need it least: the people who already have capital or access to capital.

Third, it enables the measurement of things that the current money system cannot measure. It will enable public and Social Banks to attach a value to things such as community based behavior, environmental protection and the promotion of the arts and creative expression. Individual public and Social Banks can offer social dollars to musicians, teachers, coaches, elder care providers, health care providers and others who currently are unable to convince existing banks of the value of what they provide to society.

Fourth, it is self sustaining financially. Because all transactions in social dollars are digital they can be easily tracked through the system. Whenever there is an exchange of social dollars a nominal fee will be assessed. This fee in most cases will be so small that it is unnoticeable to the user of social dollars, but in aggregate it will be fully sufficient to fund the operating expenses of the system. At scale such a fee might even be sufficient to create a pool of capital that is available to fund promising startup social enterprise or provide direct relief to those most in need.

Fifth, it is easy to regulate the amount of social flowing through The Credit Commons. If too many social dollars are flowing through the system and their value is decreasing relative to the value of government / bank generated dollars, their use can be discouraged by increasing the transaction fees, fractional reserve ratios or the negative interest rate (demurrage fee) applied to the social dollars held in accounts of Social Bank. These market based mechanisms will stabilize the value of social dollars as reflected by their price vis a vis dollars, rewards, airlines miles or points on a secondary trading market.

Money as a Form of Energy

Most people use their energy to create money, because this is what the incentives of our economic system motivate them to do. In that sense money is a form of energy. However, when one uses money just too make more money, the energy that is contained within the money is dissipated and it loses its meaning. If instead one takes the energy contained in money and passes it onto others in meaningful ways, then the meaningful potential of money is multiplied. This is the potential inherent in the social dollar, social currency, Social Banking system. It will increase the positive energy flowing throughout our society as positive energy circulating in monetary form. With social dollars flowing, the transfer of money becomes both a source of financial gain and inspiration. Conversely, if money is passed onto others with the sole intention of personal gain, then it is passed on as either neutral or negative energy. What makes the difference between money that is passed on as positive energy and money that is passed on as negative or neutral energy?"

THE WORD 'COMMUNITY' COMES FROM LATIN, MEANING 'EXCHANGING GIFTS AMONG EACH OTHER. SOME MONEY SYSTEMS CAN PRESERVE THIS GIFT MECHANISM. EXAMPLE OF MONEY SYSTEMS THAT PRESERVES THE GIFT ASPECT OF COMMUNAL ENERGY EXCHANGE ARE FORMAL SYSTEMS FOR KEEPING TRACK OF THE VALUE OF GOODS OR SERVICES EXCHANGED BETWEEN MEMBERS OF A DEFINED GROUP. THESE DIFFER FROM NATIONAL CURRENCY BECAUSE THEY ARE VALID ONLY WITHIN THE GROUP.... EVERYONE WHO CONTRIBUTES A NUMBER OF CREDITS TO THE LOCAL CURRENCY BANK CAN EXCHANGE THOSE CREDITS FOR GOODS OR SERVICES FROM OTHER MEMBERS OF THE COMMUNITY, AND MUST WORK OFF THOSE GOODS AND SERVICES BY CONTRIBUTING TO THOSE WHO HAVE NEED OF WHATEVER THEY HAVE TO OFFER.

- BERNARD LIETAER, "THE FUTURE OF MONEY"

In order for money to be multiplied as positive energy, there must be an alignment of vision, values and valuation. If an investor, lender or a donor establishes this alignment with another person, the transfer of money is a transfer of positive energy as a form of inspiration. Hence, money can either be an agent of inaction and inertia or an agent of inspiration and initiative. It all depends on the character of the energy that flows from the transfer of money.

Bringing Balance To Our Uses of Money

People don't make their economic choices consciously. Rather they go with the flow of economic incentives inherent in monetary systems and let forces they perceive to be beyond their control, govern their lives. They treat money and markets as if they were Gods that rule their lives. In good times, people have superficial feelings of happiness, because markets enable them to create wealth, without realizing that markets are not creating a true measure of meaningful value.

This can affect societies as well as individuals. If not understood, these forces can become paralyzing to entire sectors and societies. This is the nature of ascendency and decline of countries, currencies and civilizations. For a nation's strength is ultimately a reflection of the cumulative impact of all its energy and capital flows. When a nation finds itself slipping into decline and depression, there are both economic and psychological dimensions because money has become divorced from meaning. The result is crisis of confidence, malaise and a flow of negative energy throughout all sectors of society. Trust dissipates. Businesses stop expanding. People stop helping each other out. Entrepreneurs give up on their visions. Investors stop investing in innovative ideas and exceptional entrepreneurs." How then can we create an alignment between money and meaning?

Capitalism 3.0 with social dollars flowing raises to a conscious level the purposes we bring to the use of our money. When we attune our attention to the purpose our money serves, it becomes possible to bring back balance to business and to change the dynamics of economic interaction. This simple shift can changes the course of commerce and revitalize the economies that propel our way of life.

> As a material society, money is energy. The more you can be in relationship to it, the more you can be conscious about your life.
>
> - Paul Haller, Teacher of "The Dharma of Money at The San Francisco Zen Center

The Limits of Traditional Philanthropy

Philanthropists, on the whole, believe that they have a finite pool of resources and their dilemma is how to allocate those resources to do the most good. Many philanthropists are beginning to explore new models and ways of leveraging their resources, but none has yet arrived at what can be the breakthrough idea–the systemic solution to the root causes of the problems. Instead, they are all still diligently sifting through ideas and applications that at best offer the promise of putting a few more fingers in the holes of the dyke, while the onrush of the much larger tide of social, economic and environmental dislocation and devastation is looming.

Those who operate in the social economy must rely on the highly idiosyncratic judgments and intermittent largesse of those who have benefitted from the rules that only value and reward profit-motivated activity. Capital markets, today, ignore the social economy. Societies interests, preserving the natural environment and the needs of non profits and social enterprises are an afterthought at best. The public interest, which everybody should be concerned about, are only considered relevant by a few enlightened managers, and in those cases, only if the public interests serve the bottom line. Extraordinary power accrues to those who administer and manage flows of capital through financial markets: bankers, investment bankers, hedge fund managers, investment managers and other creatures of the market using leverage. Leverage is the ability to take a small amount of capital and multiply its impact either by borrowing from a financial institution or by issuing stock. Financial leverage can only be achieved when appropriate financial instruments exist to enable it. Foundations today talk about leveraging the impact of their resources through collaboration or other creative approaches, but they mostly use the term as metaphor, because without the appropriate financial instruments, financial leverage is impossible for the social economy.

Despite much talk about new models of venture philanthropy and social enterprise, no financial instruments exist today that can enable non profits to achieve financial leverage. Thus most social enterprises and non profits largely remain small entities of limited impact, while their counterparts in the private sector achieve scale and influence, while accumulating wealth and power. That wealth and power usually brings greater financial credibility, which can be further leveraged in their own self interest. Lacking financial instruments to take advantage of the phenomenon of leverage, well intentioned social entrepreneurs sometimes manage to muddle through, achieving success on a small scale, but they seldom are able to break through to a size that they can effectively address increasingly large, complex and intractable global problems.

Leveraging the Power of Doing Good

Non profits cumulatively raise almost $300 billion in charitable contributions annually. This seems like a lot of money until you compare it to the hundreds of trillions of dollars that are sloshing around global capital markets and stock exchanges. To appreciate the magnitude of the disparity in power and influence between the private sector and social sector is consider the following. The Sierra Club is generally considered to be one of the largest and most successful environmental groups in the world. The Sierra Club's annual operating budget is less than $90 million. Adam Werbach, former President of the Sierra Club, contrasts this to Walmart, where he recently worked as a consultant. Werbach points out that the total budget of the Sierra Club is less than the average budget of any one of Walmart's 2000 stores.

Capital markets are designed to exclusively serve private, profit-motivated interests. Capital markets don't even recognize any entity that is not legally organized as a profit making company. They tend to look very skeptically at any for profit entity that openly discusses its larger intentions beyond making money. Without direct access to capital markets, non profits and social entrepreneurs are seen as beggars, outcasts and starving people by the saints who are enlightened enough to recognize them lying on the streets of our society. In other words, markets have served as wondrous wealth creation mechanisms for private interests, but they have not served the social economy, the society at large or natural environment so well.

Over the last two centuries there has been a steady erosion of power with the social sector, which includes churches, educational institutions, and all manner of cultural, civic and activist groups. That erosion has transferred power towards the private sector. Just look at the skylines of the great cities of the world. The spires of churches, once the dominant structures in cities are now dwarfed by the towering skyscrapers that house the corporate interests of the private sector. During this power shift, we have seen social and environmental problems grow in severity and magnitude largely because the institutions that are creating the problems have no direct self interest in developing real solutions.

When social and green business practices can be monetized in the marketplace, companies they don't have to greenwash for PR purposes. The can jump on Green bandwagon because it will positively impact their bottom line. No longer will the corporate level of commitment towards society be circumscribed by the rigidities of narrow financial analysis. The net result will be that environmental problems and economic inequalities will no longer be outdistanced societies collective ability to deal with them.

The limitations of philanthropy and charity in their present forms are well known. With an average foundation grant near $25,000, it is unlikely that groups, no matter how well intentioned, will be able to scale to a level where a serious impact is made against the towering scale of the problems we face. This systemic change in the way money is created can begin to alter this balance of power between the private and social  sector. It will result in a fundamental power shift that will have a profoundly beneficial effect on our society. It will unleash an explosion of creative energy that will revitalize the social sector.

THE NET EFFECT IS TO INTRODUCE THE POWER OF LEVERAGE TO THE BENEFIT OF PEOPLE AND GROUPS WORKING FOR POSITIVE CHANGE, MUCH LIKE LEVERAGE TODAY BENEFITS PRIVATE COMPANIES.

The Next Great Wave of Wealth Creation

The implications of these systemic shifts go well beyond the world of banking, marketing, promotion and philanthropy. The Credit Commons will also

awaken our slumbering economy. The annual value of the wealth that can be created through the monetization of social equity is over $3 trillion. The creation of The Social Reserve Banking System will usher in a fourth great wave of wealth creation in the modern technology era, and expanding the economy without creating inflationary pressure. Consider this from the historical perspective of the three great waves of wealth creation in the modern tech sector:

> EACH OF THE FIRST THREE GREAT WAVES WAS THE RESULT OF NEW TECHNOLOGICAL TOOLS AND MECHANISMS THAT ENABLED THE MEASUREMENT AND MONETIZATION OF SOMETHING WHOSE VALUE HAD PREVIOUSLY BEEN UNRECOGNIZED, UNMEASURABLE OR UNMARKETABLE. IN THE PROCESS A VIABLE MARKET WAS CREATED WHERE THERE HAD BEEN NONE BEFORE. WE TEND TO FORGET THAT BEFORE BILL GATES AND MICROSOFT, THE MARKET ATTACHED VERY LITTLE VALUE TO THE INTELLECTUAL ENERGY AND CAPITAL THAT WENT INTO THE CREATION OF SOFTWARE.

- **Television:** The first great wave of wealth creation came not when the technology of television was developed, but rather when the Nielsen ratings were created, enabling TV networks to measure audience size and thus sell their program based content to advertisers.

- **Software:** The second great wave came not when the personal computer was developed, but rather when Bill Gates and Microsoft created a mindset and network that valued software. Before Microsoft, software had been considered a valueless commodity, although huge amounts of intellectual capital was invested in its creation.
- **The Internet:** The third great wave came not when Google developed a search engine, but rather when they developed their Adsense and Adwords programs, which enabled the monetization of Internet traffic and click throughs. This spawned the creation of a vast and complex advertising network based upon targeted keywords. We forget that before Google and Adsense, it was very difficult for Websites to derive value from the traffic they were generating.

There will come a day when people will have forgotten that social and environmental equity was once undervalued by the market, because there were no mechanism for measuring and monetizing it. The fourth great wave will come with the creation of new financial instruments, mechanisms and secondary markets that can measure and monetize the value of previously unrecognized social and environmental equity.

Significantly from a historical standpoint, this fourth great wave of wealth creation will benefit those who are working for the greater good of society. It will thereby help attenuate the economic, societal and environmental imbalances that exist under the present rules of the game. It will catalyze a fundamental shift in thinking that helps engage a broad section of our population in public or environmentally based initiatives using social dollars as financial incentives for fundamental changes that will benefit us all.

A SHORT HISTORY OF CAPITALISM

BEFORE WE CONSIDER HOW TO UPGRADE OUR ECONOMIC OPERATING SYSTEM, IT'S WORTH CONTEMPLATING HOW IT CAME TO BE. TWO PARALLEL THREADS EMERGE: THE DECLINE OF THE COMMONS AND THE ASCENT OF PRIVATE CORPORATIONS. WHEN I SPEAK IN THIS BOOK OF CORPORATIONS, I'M SPEAKING OF A VERY SPECIAL INSTITUTION: THE PUBLICLY TRADED STOCK CORPORATION.

THIS IS AN INSTITUTION WITH A BOARD OF DIRECTORS, A SET OF EXECUTIVE OFFICERS, AND A FLUCTUATING SET OF SHAREHOLDERS TO WHOM THE DIRECTORS AND OFFICERS ARE LEGALLY ACCOUNTABLE. THESE CORPORATIONS HAVE AN EXPLICIT MISSION: TO MAXIMIZE RETURN TO STOCK OWNERS. IF AN ACCOUNTING COULD BE MADE, CORPORATE APPROPRIATIONS OF THE COMMONS IN AMERICA ALONE WOULD BE WORTH TRILLIONS OF DOLLARS. WITH ONE HAND, CORPORATIONS TAKE VALUABLE STUFF FROM THE COMMONS AND PRIVATIZE IT. WITH THE OTHER HAND, THEY DUMP BAD STUFF INTO THE COMMONS AND PAY NOTHING. THEY ACT THIS WAY NOT BECAUSE THEY WANT TO, BUT BECAUSE THEY HAVE TO... SOMETIME AROUND 1950, CAPITALISM ENTERED A NEW PHASE. UNTIL THEN, POVERTY WAS A WIDELY SHARED EXPERIENCE. PEOPLE WANTED MORE GOODS THAN THE ECONOMY COULD PROVIDE. DEMAND, IN OTHER WORDS, EXCEEDED SUPPLY, AND WE LIVED IN WHAT MIGHT BE CALLED SHORTAGE CAPITALISM. WE COULD ALSO CALL IT CAPITALISM 1.0. IN THE PERIOD FOLLOWING WORLD WAR II, WE SHIFTED INTO SURPLUS CAPITALISM, OR WHAT I CALL CAPITALISM 2.0. IN THIS VERSION, THERE'S NO LIMIT TO WHAT CORPORATIONS CAN PRODUCE; THEIR PROBLEM IS FINDING BUYERS. A SIZEABLE CHUNK OF GDP IS SPENT TO MAKE PEOPLE WANT THIS UNNEEDED OUTPUT. AND CREDIT IS LAVISHLY EXTENDED SO THEY CAN BUY IT. THIS HISTORIC SHIFT CAN BE DESCRIBED ANOTHER WAY. A CENTURY AGO, OUR CHIEF SCARCITY WAS GOODS. IT THUS MADE SENSE TO SACRIFICE OTHER THINGS IN PURSUIT OF GOODS, AND CAPITALISM WAS MASTERFUL AT DOING THIS. TODAY OUR SCARCITIES ARE DIFFERENT. AMONG THE MIDDLE CLASSES, THE TOP SCARCITIES, I'D SAY, ARE TIME, COMPANIONSHIP, AND COMMUNITY. AMONG THE POOR, THERE REMAINS A LACK OF GOODS, BUT THAT LACK ISN'T DUE TO A SHORTAGE OF PRODUCTION CAPACITY—IT'S DUE TO THE POOR'S INABILITY TO PAY. THE CRITICAL SCARCITY HERE, IN OTHER WORDS, IS INCOME. SIMILARLY, IN THE EARLY CAPITALIST ERA, LAND, RESOURCES, AND PLACES TO DUMP WASTES WERE ABUNDANT; AGGREGATED CAPITAL WAS THE SCARCEST FACTOR. THAT'S WHY RULES AND PRACTICES DEVELOPED THAT PUT CAPITAL ABOVE ALL ELSE. IN THE TWENTY-FIRST CENTURY, HOWEVER, THIS IS NO LONGER THE CASE.

- PETER BARNES, AUTHOR: CAPITALISM 3.0 - A GUIDE TO RECLAIMING THE COMMONS

An Operating System for the Social Economy

Think of the global economy as a computer. Today all computers have an operating system, which provides a set of functions designed to efficiently allocate the computer's processing power to the various competing applications. The closest thing the global economy has to an operating system is the market. In this analogy, the private corporations of the world are like applications that appeal to capital markets for resources not unlike a computers various applications come to the

operating system looking for processing power.

Market evangelists vigorously argue that markets make sound and efficient decisions in allocating resources. Are these resource allocations really so beneficial in a larger societal and environmental context, when capital markets don't even recognize entities that are not legally or philosophically constituted as for profit?

The way global markets allocate resources is like a computer's operating system that refuses to directly allocate any processing power to whole classes of functions that are vital to the effective operation of the computer. It's as if, when you seek to save your work, the computer sends you an error message saying, *"This computer does not recognize this command. If you wish to save your work, you must first persuade another application to allocate some of its processing power to this function. Unfortunately, other applications may not understand the value of saving your work. They may think your work is really stupid and has been a big waste of time. Thus, they may not choose to give up any of their processing power to you. The choice is theirs and theirs alone. So we suggest that you ask very nicely and craft your appeal carefully so that it is tailored to the predisposed ideas of those other applications you are asking. Good luck."*

Since the social economy operates without capital markets or any centralized sharing mechanisms, it's essentially functioning like a computer without an operating system. There are 1.5 million applications that are vying for the scarce resources of the computer and there is no efficient or rational way for the computer (philanthropists) to decide how to prioritize or allocate those resources. Hence most foundations and philanthropists find themselves in situations where they seek to meet with as many potentials beneficiaries as possible, but the process is haphazard, scattered, frustrating, time consuming, costly, draining and inefficient.

As long as capital markets exclusively serve private economy and ignore the social economy, imbalances will continue to become more pronounced. Social and environmental problems will continue to grow in magnitude, complexity and intractability until eventually we reach a point of reckoning.

Stabilizing The System

The net effect of this new system will be to act as a flywheel to stabilize the existing financial system. How? Social dollars will target those in greatest need and make it less likely that they will default on their mortgages and loans and credit cards. Yet, the effects of this system will be even more profound. In this Social Banking system, with the power to create money in a decentralized and democratized manner, the system will enable those social enterprises that acting in the public interest. It will facilitate their access to capital to finance their needs and scale their visions. This is an idea whose time has come.

This Social Banking system will give hope to millions of American citizens who now live in perpetual debt and fear of their financial future. It will accomplish the same ends you seek to achieve with your stimulus package without incurring mounting risks associated with growing governmental debt. It's a timely and systemic solution to our economic crisis that will speak to the needs of all manner of groups that are currently starved of the capital they need to address society's interest without incurring governmental debt.

For such a system to come into being government must embrace an unprecedented level of collaboration with the social and private sectors. It's an unprecedented opportunity that grows out of an unprecedented crisis. As you stand on the stage of history, please give it serious thought. Your role in history will be defined by your willingness to embrace change. This is the type of systemic change you promised in your inspirational campaign for President. Will you make good on your promise? The future of America rests in the balance.

Scaling Social Programs

To address increasingly large and intractable social and environmental problems we need to focus on capital resource allocation. On one extreme are small grants and loans to relatively small non profits and social entrepreneurs. At the other extreme are gargantuan hedge funds that derive much of their economic power from their access to capital markets. Hedge funds, and private equity firms aggressively use leverage to acquire equity stakes in private companies, usually only putting only a fraction of the purchase price down as cash. The rest comes as debt or equity financial instruments. Leverage as a financial idea is not available to the social sector because there are no financial instruments that can be leveraged by non profits.

Can we enable social sector organizations to scale their programs using the same kinds of financial leverage that the private sector uses to scale their programs? Yes we can! Social dollars will be used to incentivize all kinds of behavior that are in society's interest. For example a school, that has become certified as a Social Bank will be empowered to issue social dollars as incentives for excellence in teaching, administration or studies. An environmental group will be empowered as a Social Bank to issue social dollars as incentives for energy conservation, carpooling or adoption of renewable energy sources. A senior citizen center will be empowered to issue social dollars to elders to encourage them get involved in social causes or encourage volunteers to spend time with elders assisting them with projects. A hospital or health center will be empowered to issue social dollars for various preventive health measures. The applications of this kind of "social currency" will only be limited by the imagination of those who were using it.

In the process a mechanism has been created for the measurement and monetization of social equity. Suddenly the social sector is no longer operating in a sphere unto itself, but it has financial instruments for wealth creation that is based not on the intention of private gain, but rather on the intention of public benefit or social improvement. It's a systemic shift of power, that starts to create sustainable income sources for the social sector using the same kind of leverage that the private sector uses to create wealth. It can have a pervasive impact on our society enabling us to address problems in a way never before considered possible. It will engage a broad cross section of our population by integrating their participation into the fabric of mainstream commerce, culture and community. The entity that creates it must be composed of people who inspire trust with the general public and have broad representation from the existing networks that today comprise from the social sector. In a sense, it will be a network of networks that is able to effectively synthesize the goodwill of many other non profit communities and networks. How might this system be created and implemented? What financial structure will support it?

The Time is Ripe for a Bold Vision

The time is ripe for a bold vision for systemic solutions to systemic problems. That can only happen when we find a way to tap the huge power of existing financial markets and channel it towards the solutions of problems. These are ambitious and visionary ideas, but they are not wild or unrealistic. We must remember the context in which they are put forth. Our society today is on the brink of major environmental economic and social calamities. Absent systemic change that address the root causes of our problems, we are facing adjustments and hardships. We can only imagine how severe those adjustments might be.

Today, there is broad recognition in very high places that something must be done and done quickly. Discussions of possible reforms are taking place regularly in forums like the Davos conference, The Clinton Global Initiative, The Skoll Foundation's annual conference on Social Entrepreneurship, The Bill and Melinda Gates Foundation, The Omidyar Foundation, and boardrooms across the corporate spectrum. There is now a widespread acceptance of urgency in addressing global problems.

We can be confident that the ingenuity and creativity now in full force in the buildout of the social enterprise field and Web 2.0 technologies, is fully sufficient to meet any challenges that await us. At colleges and business schools across the country there is palpable interest in joining companies that are committed to something more than making money for their shareholders. *The Credit Commons* involves a fundamental rethinking of arguably the most powerful tool ever devised by humans: money. It implementation will require the cooperation of businesses large and small, banks and financial institutions, schools and universities, governments, foundations, non profits and social enterprises. While the scope of the challenge is daunting, it can be systematically structured and introduced through pilot programs that enable the fine tuning of the ideas incrementally.

Today even the most powerful are searching for answers and recognize that it is in their own self interest to provide some from of relief to those struggling to survive economically.

Addressing Problems at Their Root

As the built in dynamics of the market based economy magnify income inequalities, meeting this challenge grows ever more imperative, Whether we are talking about the meltdown of the mortgage markets and the increasing defaults on credit cards in the United States, or the deprivation of villagers in Sub Sahara Africa, we can no longer ignore the consequences of income disparities. In an increasingly interconnected global economy, the fate people at the bottom is increasingly relevant to the fate of people at the top.

If we fail to recognize the root causes of the problems, those people who join social motivated organizations will still find themselves frustrated by lack of sufficient resources. Until we develop structural means to facilitate scaling of good ideas, our best efforts will only be nibbling at the edges of the problems. We need to find better ways to allocate resources so that the social economy is no longer starved

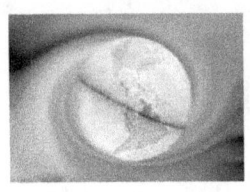 of the resources they need to serve society. Ultimately, we must focus on our common interests. We must act now and with great urgency make the overall economy more stable, balanced and equitable by open up new capital sources, create new mechanisms, develop new financial instruments and markets to serve the social economy in the same way that existing capital market serve the private economy.

The Credit Commons will enable the measurement and monetization of things that the market based economy currently ignores. The social dollars social currency will attach a tangible value to social and public spirited activity and thereby create lasting and powerful incentives for business enterprise and individuals to address social and environmental problems. In a sense, the social dollars social currency is a "Cap and Trade" system for valuing social equity. But it's implications are much more profound since it reaches into all aspects of our society, not just energy.

The benefits of this new Social Banking, social investment and social monetary system will be far reaching and profound. The system will mitigate the risks inherent in the current banking system, by helping to recycle money to the people in greatest need thus helping to reduce default rates. Social dollars will awaken the overall economy in a way that quick fix stimulus plans, fiscal and monetary policy cannot. It will establish a mechanism to monetize the value of the estimate 2 trillion dollars of community based, environmental, non profit, volunteer and family building activity that is currently unrecognized by the market based economy. In sum, these structural changes will catalyze a new wave of wealth creation for the entire economy while strengthening the bonds of community. It's a long-term, market-based solution to our current financial crisis.

A Trim Tab To Change Direction

The Credit Commons will create a fundamental shift that adjusts the structural imbalances that grow out of out current market based economy. It will make it easier for those who have chosen a course to help society through non profit work or creative expression, to survive economically by creating a mechanism for the monetization of the social equity they have created or accumulated. It will also making it easier for people in both groups to create connections, and find the resources they need to prosper and grow through social marketing relationships, social finance arrangements. In so doing it will empower everyone, bring meaning to people's lives and sustenance to their dreams.

> WE ARE NOT GOING TO BE ABLE TO OPERATE OUR SPACESHIP EARTH SUCCESSFULLY NOR FOR MUCH LONGER UNLESS WE SEE IT AS A WHOLE SPACESHIP AND OUR FATE AS COMMON. IT HAS TO BE EVERYBODY OR NOBODY.
> - R BUCKMINSTER FULLER

Futurist Buckminster Fuller introduced the idea of the "Trimtab factor." A trimtab, is a small rudder affixed to the rudder of the great ship that can be adjusted ever so slightly to alter course in a fundamental way. This Social Banking system will be that trimtab, that can alter the course of the global economy, if we only have the courage, vision and ingenuity to take a chance on it. This systemic adjustment as "Trimtab" will be affixed to the rudder of the great ship we call the global economy, enabling a shift away from the reckoning that awaits us on our present course.

Pay It Forward

The Credit Commons builds on the "Pay it Forward" idea by introducing the power of financial leverage into the DNA of the social economy. In this way, it will create a bridge between the world of banking and the world of philanthropy. This will reduce the crushing debt loads of state and federal government and reduce the taxpayer money flowing abroad to investors and lender from Asia, Europe and the middle East.

This is a way to systemically moderate the instabilities and inequities of our current banking and monetary system without incurring destabilizing levels of governmental debt. This parallel Social Banking system will catalyze the creation of

a "community of trust" composed of the millions of people who recognize that there is something fundamentally wrong with a financial system that only rewards profit making activity to the exclusion of important social, equity, health, community based and environmental concerns. These new Social Bank will help decentralize and democratize the banking system and insure that no one bank is "too big to fail." It will democratize the power to create money and restore balance to our economy because these new Social Banks will represent the larger constituencies than are served by our existing banking system. Social Banks will provide relief to those at the bottom of the economic ladder, thereby stabilizing the primary banking system.

Existing and widely respected institutions such as universities, schools, social enterprises, corporations, churches, community groups, non profits and others can apply to become Social Banks. Government agencies (national, state and local) can also become public banks, as well as entirely new institutions formed for special purposes to address pressing social, heath related or environmental needs. The certification process will include an articulation of some social, economic or environmental purpose for their use of social dollars. Once certified, they will be empowered to create money as either dollars or social dollars, just as commercial banks today create money when they extend credit.

> THROUGH THEIR BLIND AND UNCONDITIONAL FAITH IN THE FINANCIAL MARKETS, THE BANKS AND THE GOVERNMENT HAVE MADE US ALL INTO VICTIMS OF GREED GONE OUT OF CONTROL. THIS CRISIS IS AN OPPORTUNITY FOR PRESIDENT OBAMA TO LEAD THE U.S. IN A NEW DIRECTION; ONE THAT VALUES ECONOMIC GROWTH, BUT PROTECTS THE WELL-BEING OF THE PUBLIC BEFORE THE BANK ACCOUNTS OF THE WORLD'S FINANCIAL ELITE.
> — HTTP://ANEWWAYFORWARD.ORG/BLOG/

This system will introduce and expand the use of a new social currency called, "social dollars." Social dollars be exchanged against dollars on a secondary exchange. They can also be exchanged against private currencies like airline miles, rewards and point systems – all at floating rates. They also will be convertible into the thousands of complementary currencies that are operating in communities around the world. In addition, they can be used while shopping to obtain discounts, reduced interest rates and other incentives from a vast network of corporate and citizen partners who become part of a "community of trust" that recognizes the need to moderate the inequities, instabilities and imbalances of our current financial system.

> "NEITHER THE ADMINISTRATION, NOR OUR POLITICAL SYSTEM IN GENERAL, IS READY TO FACE UP TO THE FACT THAT WE'VE BECOME A SOCIETY IN WHICH THE BIG BUCKS GO TO BAD ACTORS, A SOCIETY THAT LAVISHLY REWARDS THOSE WHO MAKE US POORER. THE ADMINISTRATION ... SEEMS TO OPERATE ON THE PRINCIPLE THAT WHAT'S GOOD FOR WALL STREET IS GOOD FOR AMERICA."
>
> — NOBEL PRIZE WINNING ECONOMIST, PAUL KRUGMAN

Our Wake Up Call

Crises have always been moments to rethink existing systems. Perhaps, just perhaps the severity of our financial crisis, coming as it does at a time of broad acceptance of the severity of the climate change crisis and a time of political change, this is the perfect storm we need to put a system in place that will enable us to move into a new, more stable and more equitable phase of capitalism.

The Credit Commons is both achievable and of transformative power. This parallel money system will be embraced by a wide array of social enterprises, non profit groups, schools, foundations, agencies, cultural and civic groups. Why? Simple economics. The system democratizes financial power. It extends power to create money. Ultimately, creating *The Credit Commons* is an exercise is expanding trust. By creating an ever expanding community of trust, we can lift ourselves up, seize control of our financial future, stimulate the economy and build a hopeful future together by democratizing the power to create money.

So THE QUESTION BEFORE US IS THIS: WILL OUR CURRENT ECONOMIC, SOCIAL AND ENVIRONMENTAL CRISES SERVE AS A WAKE UP CALL, SUFFICIENTLY SCARY, THAT WE RECOGNIZE THE NEED TO WORK TOGETHER, THINKING IN FUNDAMENTAL TERMS ABOUT LONG TERM, SYSTEMIC AND SUSTAINABLE SOLUTIONS THAT ADDRESS THE ROOT CAUSES OF OUR PREDICAMENT? WHAT PATH WILL WE CHOOSE TO THE FUTURE? THE CHOICE IS OURS. THE FATE OF AMERICA LIES IN THE BALANCE.

An Inflection Point in History

We are at an inflection point in history. With "The Movement" now unfolding on the streets, the media, the conferences and small gatherings across the country, we have thrust ourselves onto the world's stage at a moment of unprecedented economic crisis. While President Obama and other politicians continue to rely on the advice of economic "experts" they have become wedded to a financial system that concentrates, and centralizes economic power with commercial banks. They have rolled the dice in a huge gamble based upon hope: hope to jump start the economy, hope to revitalize the financial system and hope to rebuild the American Dream. The stakes are huge. The fate of America now rests upon the success of their gambit.

What if it doesn't work? The combined commitments of federal agencies to bail out financial institutions and stimulate the economy now approaches $12 trillion. This is an astounding level of risk. This strategy creates potential public liabilities exceeding the entire national debt. In essence you have jeopardized the solvency of the U. S. government on this gamble, with no alternative in place.

There an alternative to this grim scenario? If we truly want to be the champion of change and awaken our economy in a meaningful way, then we need to consider an alternative approach that creates alternative forms of liquidity in the financial system. The *"Credit Commons."* is one approach. There are others. We can construct an infrastructure of new decentralized, public purpose and Social Banks that are empowered to create money just the way commercial banks today create money.

Protecting
Our Commons

NEVER DOUBT THAT A SMALL
GROUP OF COMMITTED CITIZENS
CAN CHANGE THE WORLD.
INDEED, IT'S THE ONLY THING
THAT EVER HAS.
- MARGARET MEAD

A Prophesy About the Coming Revolution

Two years ago, anticipating the coalescence of a movement that today is taking the form of Occupy Wall Street, I let my imagination take me into the future and penned, a somewhat whimsical and, it turns out, quite prophetic work of fiction: **The Wiz of Iz: a Prophesy About the Coming Revolution**. That book is about an inchoate movement led by a metaphorical leader who represents hope for change.... and the movement grows virally using modern technology. The book is also about the role of technology layered upon widespread popular discontent with the status quo of economic inequality.

The Wiz of Iz is a prophesy in the form of a powerful parable – a story where the characters represent something much more than who they are. The Wiz of Iz is a modern day version of The Wizard of Oz, a story many believe was written as a parable about the world of money and banking?

We're now living through an epochal period of change, though most people are too busy to realize what's really going on. We need to understand the root causes of these changes and we need vehicle to invite participation in ways that are peaceful, creative, non threatening - even playful. The tactics of the Occupy Movement have some of these characteristics.

The world is at an inflection point in history and we need to understand what's really happening to the culture and institutions that influence our lives. We need a common story to help understand what we're all going through. The Wiz of Iz contains a powerful truth in the form of a big idea. This idea, like a philosophers stone, must be viewed from different angles to behold it in all its splendor. This idea is seen from diverse perspectives through the prism of the Ten Traces of Truth inscribed on the Tablet of Truth. It relates to the most powerful tool ever created by humans–MONEY.

Today the meaning of money is finding its way into the our economic equation with the blending of emerging trends like social enterprise, social media, clean technology, slow money, free banking, virtual currency, cybercash, mobile payments, renewable energy, venture philanthropy, micro-finance, complementary currencies, green marketing, socially responsible investing and other trends that have not yet been labeled. Most of these ideas still operate at the periphery of our economy, but they're moving towards the mainstream.

Yet even as these emerging values grow in significance, they have not yet been ingrained into the code of money itself. That moment is fast approaching and when it happens, this movement will move into the forefront of our consciousness. It's an inevitable stage in the ongoing evolution of money and money systems. The code we program into the design of our money and our money systems is the strongest motivational force ever devised by humans. Money holds a mysterious power over our lives - a power so great it either push entire nations to the brink of collapse or inspire an their economic awakening. It can concentrate financial power in a few hands or democratize economic power. It can create new waves of wealth creation benefitting all of society or cause convulsions of economic instability that cause pain for everyone. It can stimulate prosperity or cause a contraction of business. It can raise hopes or dash dreams.

THE WIZ OF IZ

A PROPHESY
ABOUT THE COMING
REVOLUTION

$

BOOK II

THE MEANING OF
MONEY

JOHN F. INCE

Modern technology today offers us amazing new possibilities in the way we create, use and share our money. The key to unlocking the higher potential of money is new thinking about a new kind money–a more Meaningful Money that incorporates a new consciousness that might be called the Code of Common Cents.

We need a story that proffers insight into the nature of the crisis we're going through and enables us to draw something powerful out of the depths of our collective soul. In times of economic crisis, and there is a real need for the uplift of bold new ideas, but change won't come from use smoke and mirrors to mask real problems. It won't come from quick fixes, used to avoid long term problems. Genuine change only comes when we advance our thinking into new and more fertile fields of discussion: fields where value and values are merged in new kind of marketplace.

The plot of The Wiz of Iz roughly follows the plot of The Wizard of Oz. A cast of allegorical figures from The Land of Iz, find themselves lost in a land of negativity called The Land of Izn't controlled by the Deputies of the Demon of Darkness. These intrepid souls want to return to their Land of Iz, but are told that they must first find Ten Truths which taken together constitute the Tablet of Truth. These characters follow the Rainbow Road where they meet elders, experts and eccentrics, who each provide a trace of truth which must be piece together into the Tablet of Truth before the Switch of Significance can be flipped and a Common Cents Code embedded into the Meaningful Money System. will take hold. Each in their own way is seeking empowerment to contend with the crises they face. They too hope that The Wiz of Iz can help them "flip the Switch of Significance" to create change we need. Sound familiar? All this, of course, is a literary vehicle for exploring the future dimensions of our current economic, environmental, spiritual and social crises in a way that invites reader enjoyment without burden of heavy ideas and dense economic theories. Author's Preface

We're in the midst of historic economic, political and ecological crises. We need to at least consider the possibility that these crises stem from systemic flaws that will require systemic solutions. In The Wiz of Iz, I included a new Declaration of Independence, adapted from the original by just changing a few words. It's really quite amazing how timely that document is today more that 200 years after it was written.

A revolution is coming and
… it's just Common Cents.

A New Declaration of Independence

Adapted from the original text of the Declaration of Independence by The Wiz of Iz

Adopted by the Unanimous Declaration of The Insurgents of Iz

When, in the course of human events, it becomes necessary for the people to adjust the economic binds which have connected them with the oppressive systems, and to assume among the powers of the people, the ability to build separate and equal operating systems to which the laws of nature and of nature's God entitle them, a decent respect to the opinions of mankind requires that they should declare the causes which impel them to the change the existing code of the operating system for the economy .

We hold these truths to be self-evident, that all men and women are created with equal economic opportunity, that they are endowed by their Creator with certain unalienable rights, that among these are life, financial liberty and the pursuit of economic happiness. That to secure these rights, operating systems for the global economy are instituted among men and women, deriving their just economic powers from the consent and cooperation of the common citizens. That whenever any form of operating system becomes destructive to these ends, it is the right of the people to withdraw their support, and to write a new Code of Common Cents, laying its foundation on such principles and organizing newer, and more equitable systems in such form, as to them shall seem most likely to effect their financial safety and economic happiness.

Prudence, indeed, will dictate that code of the global operating system, long established should not be changed for light and transient causes; and accordingly all experience hath shown that humans are more disposed to suffer, while evils are sufferable, than to right themselves by altering the forms to which they are accustomed. But when a long train of abuses and usurpations, pursuing invariably the same objective of economic advantage and unjust financial gain, evinces a design to reduce them under absolute economic despotism, it is their right, it is their duty, to alter such code, and to program a new code that guards their future economic security.

Such has been the patient sufferance of the citizens of the land; and such is now the necessity which constrains them to alter the code of existing systems. The history of the financial oppression is a history of repeated economic injuries and economic usurpations, all having in direct object the establishment of economic injustice. To prove this, let facts about the operators of these oppressive financial systems be submitted to a candid world.

• They have refused their assent to laws, the most wholesome and necessary for the public good.

• They have lobbied legislatures to pass laws creating immediate and pressing advantage for their operations.

• They have refused to accommodate their customers and clients, unless those people would pay exorbitant interest rates and excessive fees hidden in the fine print tyrannical agreements.

• They have called together legislators at places of unusual luxury and comfort, for the sole purpose of plying them with favors and campaign contributions seeking to entice them into compliance with their measures.

• They have intimidated elected representatives and government regulators repeatedly, for opposing with manly firmness their invasions on the unjust advantages of their station.

• They have refused for a long time, to return to the people at large the economic power to which they are entitled; the government remaining in the meantime exposed to all the economic dangers of financial crisis from foreign creditors, and convulsions within.

• They have endeavored to restrict credit allocation to the people of the land; for that purpose obstructing the free flow of capital for their own selfish purposes of financial appropriation of government issued bailout funds.

• They have obstructed the administration of justice by refusing to assent to laws for establishing regulatory powers.

• They have made elected officials dependent on their will, for the tenure of their offices, and the amount and payment of campaign contributions.

• They have erected a multitude of new artifices, and sent hither swarms of self serving experts, armed with manufactured arguments, press releases and distortions of fact, to manipulate public opinion, and eat away at the substance of truth.

• They have kept among us, in times of financial crisis, standing armies of financial engineers, number crunchers and wily persuaders in order to win the consent of our legislature for government bailouts towards their own selfish financial ends.

• They have affected to render the their own political powers independent of and superior to the power of the citizens.

• They have combined with others to subject us to a jurisdiction foreign sources of capital that places foreign creditors in a superior position to the citizens of the nation and our elected representatives.

We have warned them from time to time of attempts by their legislature to extend an unwarrantable jurisdiction over us. We have reminded them of the circumstances of our emigration and settlement here. We have appealed to their native justice and magnanimity, and we have conjured them by the ties of our common kindred to disavow these usurpations, which, would inevitably interrupt our connections and correspondence. They too have been deaf to the voice of justice and of consanguinity.

We, therefore, the people of the Land of Iz, do solemnly publish and declare, that these united people are, and of right ought to be free and independent of these economic oppressors; and that as free and independent people, we have full power to create new Common Cents Code that will establish our own economic independence.

And for the support of this declaration, with a firm reliance on The Wiz of Iz, we mutually pledge to each other our lives, our Meaningful Moneeey and our sacred honor.

About the Author - John F. Ince

John F. Ince is an author, social entrepreneur, journalist, blogger, podcaster, video producer, photographer and documentary filmmaker. He is founder / CEO of The Credit Commons and  Moneeey, Inc.. He previously worked as a reporter for *Fortune Magazine*, as a contributing editor with *Upside Magazine* and as a casewriter at Harvard Business School and Harvard's John F. Kennedy School of Government. Before that he worked for Sea Pines Company and on Wall Street with Chase Manhattan Bank. He served as an aide to former Senator Paul Tsongas organizing a U.S. Senate caucus for solar energy. He has founded two non profits, One World Inc. and The Earth Aid Foundation. He is the author of The Earth Pledge and organized the Earth Pledge Campaign in conjunction with the 25th anniversary celebration of Earth Day. He is an honors graduate of Harvard College where he was First Marshal (President) of his graduating class. He received his MBA from Harvard Business School in Finance.

For those interested in learning more about how the ideas presented in this book will work in practice, please read John Ince's companion books in his social capital series:

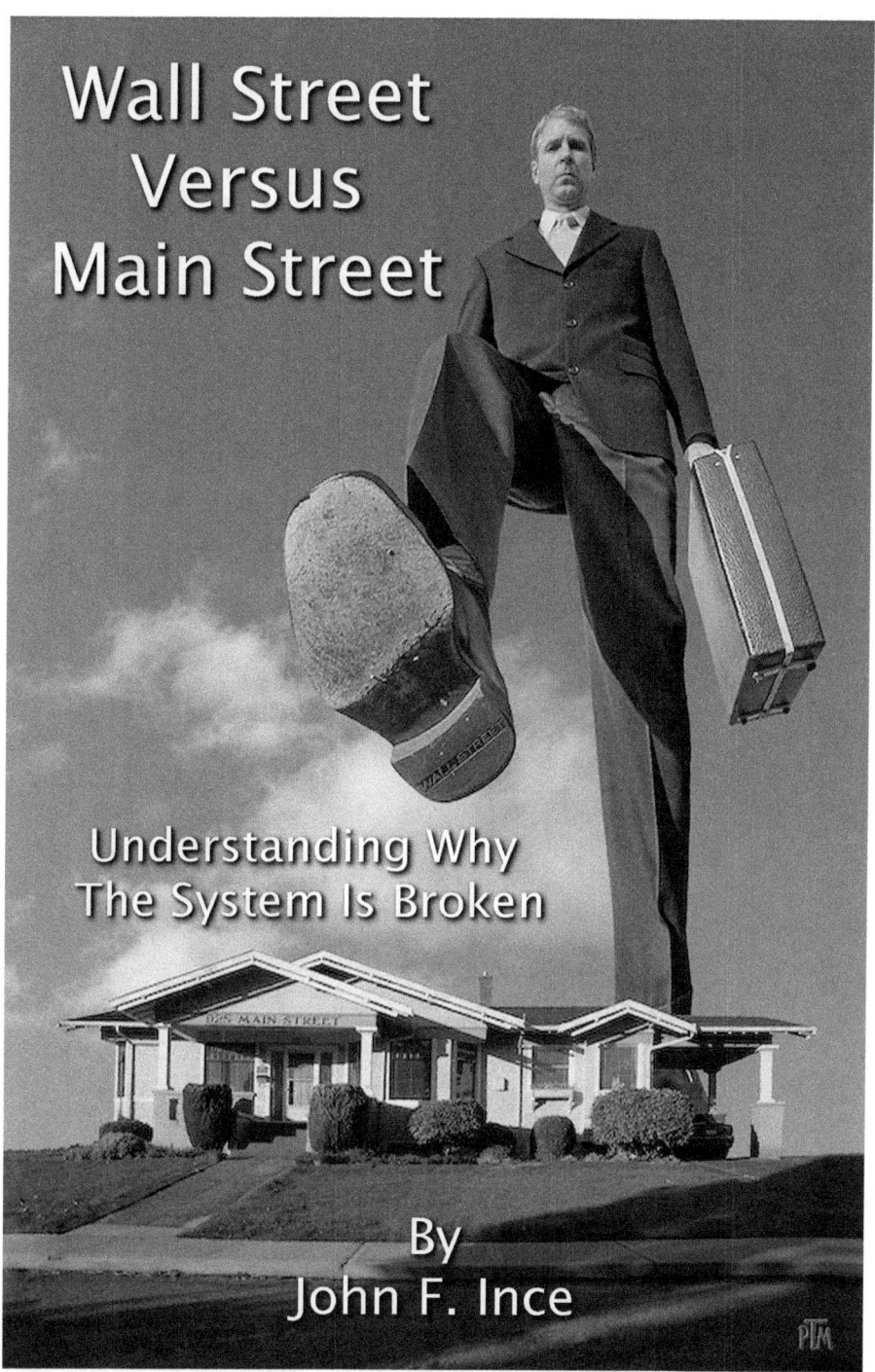

Wall Street Versus Main Street

Understanding Why The System Is Broken

By
John F. Ince

COMMON CENTS

NEW MONEY VS OLD MONEY
AND THE NEXT AMERICAN

REVOLUTION

JOHN F. INCE

Meaningful

MONEY

INNOVATION AT THE
INTERSECTION OF ...

MONEY, MEANING
AND MARKETS

JOHN F. INCE

***

To join with others concerned about
general issues
raised in this book visit:
www.MSVWS.net

To join a conversation about The Credit
Commons visit:
www.CreditCommons.net

To ask questions of the Author email:
jince@WSVMS.com

For additional copies of this book visit:
www. MSVWS.com

To read John F. Ince's blog visit:
www. johnince.com

To follow John Ince on Twitter visit:
http://twitter.com/Johnince

For additional information or
for discounts on bulk orders of this
book email:

Info@ MSVWS.com

***